PRAISE FOR *FAITHFULLY YOURS*

"Blissfully engaging and full of love, *Faithfully Yours* beautifully conveys the connection between animals and their people. A heartwarming must-read for anyone who has experienced the power of this bond."

—DR. MARTY BECKER, DVM, *"America's Veterinarian,"* Chief Veterinary Correspondent of the American Humane Association, founding member of Core Team Oz for *The Dr. Oz Show*

"More than simply a collection of heartwarming animal stories, *Faithfully Yours* gives us the chance to experience the courage, compassion, joy, and raw wonder that can happen when humans and animals find kinship. Many of Peggy Frezon's powerful tales carry long after the last page is turned."

—SUSANNAH CHARLESON, author of *Scent of the Missing: Love and Partnership with a Search and Rescue Dog* and *The Possibility Dogs: What a Handful of Rescues Taught Me About Service, Hope, and Healing*

"Enlightening. *Faithfully Yours* masterfully illuminates the spiritual connection between all animals. I loved it!"

—JENNIFER SKIFF, author of *The Divinity of Dogs* and *God Stories*

"Peggy is the real deal. She knows how animals can transform a life because her life has been transformed by the animals she loves. She also knows just how to write about those changed lives."

—RICK HAMLIN, author of *10 Prayers You Can't Live Without*

"Peggy Frezon's new book, *Faithfully Yours*, celebrates the bond between the animals who protect, serve, and heal us and the people who love them, a bond that reaches across the divide of species. These amazing true stories are sure to fascinate and inspire you."

—EDWARD GRINNAN, Editor-in-Chief, *Guideposts* magazine

FAITHFULLY
YOURS

PEGGY FREZON

FAITHFULLY YOURS

The Amazing Bond Between Us
and the Animals We Love

PARACLETE PRESS
BREWSTER, MASSACHUSETTS

2015 First Printing

Faithfully Yours: The Amazing Bond Between Us and the Animals We Love

Copyright © 2015 by Peggy Frezon

ISBN 978-1-61261-602-5

"The Doggy Diet" by Peggy Frezon originally appeared in *Guideposts* magazine and is reprinted with permission. Copyright © 2008 by Guideposts. All rights reserved.

"A Dog's Nose Knows How to Sniff Out Disease" by Peggy Frezon originally appeared on Guideposts.org.

"Mission Pawsible" by Peggy Frezon originally appeared on Guideposts.org.

"Making the Rounds" by Peggy Frezon is reproduced with permission from *Guideposts*, Guideposts.org. Copyright © 2013 by Guideposts. All rights reserved.

"My Patty Pat" by Lisa and Tom Russo originally appeared in the book *Miracles and Animals*. Copyright © 2008 by Peggy Frezon, reprinted with permission from *Guideposts*, and also appeared in the book *Kids and the Animals Who Love Them.* Copyright © 2011 by Linda and Allen Anderson. Reprinted with permission from New World Library. www.NewWorldLibrary.com.

"Homeless Homer" is based on a true account. The names and some of the details are changed to protect privacy.

The Paraclete Press name and logo (dove on cross) is a trademark of Paraclete Press, Inc.

Library of Congress Cataloging-in-Publication Data

Frezon, Peggy.
  Faithfully yours : the amazing bond between us and the animals we love / Peggy Frezon.
    pages cm
  Includes bibliographical references.
  ISBN 978-1-61261-602-5
  1. Pets. 2. Human-animal relationships. I. Title.
  SF416.F74 2015
  636.088'7—dc23   2015014125

10 9 8 7 6 5 4 3 2 1

Published by Paraclete Press
Brewster, Massachusetts
www.paracletepress.com
Printed in the United States of America

To Mike, Kelly, and Ike

CONTENTS

INTRODUCTION

Just behind the front door, an extraordinary welcome awaits.

As soon as you leave your home, anticipation of your return begins. Furry legs pace across the floor. Maybe they move to a window lookout. Keen ears perk, seeking sounds uniquely yours. Dogs can distinguish the sound of your car from the sports car across the street or the truck that rattles down the road. They can differentiate the beat of your particular shoes from the tap of high heels or the thump of work boots.

As you approach, your dog's head lifts. Ears perk.

You draw nearer. Your keys jingle! The doorknob rattles!

By now, your dog is dancing, paws leaving the ground, waiting for the door to crack open, wider and wider. When you walk over the threshold, your dog pushes forward, tail wagging and entire body wiggling as if to say, I can't believe you're finally home! I've been waiting for you forever! You're the best person in the whole wide world! I'm so happy to see you! Your dog jumps up and covers your face with kisses. Even if you've only been away a few minutes, you receive the same joyful reception. That's the kind of welcome a person rarely expects, but one dog is happy to deliver every day.

Now it's your turn. You release the day's burdens, your smile broadens. You scratch behind his ears, rub his belly, your own tension escaping through your fingertips. Then you say those words your dog has been longing to hear. "Who's a good boy?" "Who's my big girl?" You throw your arms wide and your dog jumps into your embrace. This is the best part—love flows both ways.

The American Veterinary Medical Association defines the human-animal bond as "a mutually beneficial and dynamic relationship between people and animals that is influenced by behaviors that are essential to the health and well-being of both." We love animals and feel connected to them in the same way that they love and feel connected to us.

The oldest evidence of this was found in Israel: a 12,000-year-old human skeleton with its hand resting on the skeleton of a six-month-old wolf pup. This likely shows that the wolf was a loyal pet, not an enemy.

The Human Animal Bond Score is a system created by Alice Villalobos, DVM, to rank the degree to which people feel loyal to animals. According to her, five factors come into play: (1) attachment, or the degree of bonding the person has with the animal; (2) the devotion we feel toward them, or the amount of time and effort we spend on them; (3) the value (financial or emotional) we place on them; (4) the concern we feel for their welfare; and (5) the responsibility we take toward them. Animals who rank the highest are those with two-way interaction, such as companion animals. These are animals who are regarded as best friends and family members. We value them highly and feel a high level of devotion, concern for their welfare, and responsibility toward them.

At the most basic level, humans are masters and animals serve us—as beasts of burden and farm laborers. Dogs and cats earn their keep by providing protection and pest control. Other animals may be partners, working in the military and on police forces. Animals may provide mobility and independence to people with special needs. Today, pets are cherished companions and a part of the family. We go beyond simply providing basic care of food and shelter, ever-mindful of animals' physical and emotional needs as well.

Why do we love our animals so much? Maybe it's because they surprise us with their capacity to feel, to offer us their very best and expect nothing in return. Animals accept us, protect us, comfort and heal us. They reflect the pure love of the Creator, the one who—just as our dogs blissfully bestow their unbridled reception at the front door—waits for us in anticipation, and greets us with arms wide open, dancing for joy at the sight of our faces. We love animals because they inspire us to be better humans. Aren't we lucky that they love us, too?

CHAPTER 1
DEVOTION

I'll do anything for you

The dog sat whimpering on our doorstep.
His face was beagle, his body Labrador retriever, his legs basset
hound. He'd been abandoned in the woods, every rib protruding
like slats on an old barrel. To most, he probably wasn't much to
look at—caked in dirt, patchy fur clinging to his bones. And yet,
my five-year-old self saw something quite different. "He's beautiful!" I cried, running to him and throwing my arms around his
neck. His physical appearance didn't register in my young mind
at all—his *dogness* was all I perceived. I hugged him tight. No matter how tired, how hungry, no matter what he'd been through or
how long he'd been on his own, he responded in the most canine
way—his tail pattered against the ground. His gentle tongue
kissed my cheek.

"Let's name him Happy," I said, and my family laughed because the name seemed opposite to what life had dealt him. I knew better.

There wasn't a soul Happy didn't like, but he *loved* me. He sat under the table by my feet at breakfast and followed at my heels when I went outside to play. He curled in a tight donut on my bed at night as I said my prayers. We were best friends from kindergarten through high school. Every day when I came home from school, I ran right to Happy and took him outside to chase a ball. I was as devoted to him as he was devoted to me.

Summers growing up, I lived at a church camp in the Vermont mountains. My mom worked as camp nurse. Happy walked with me down the dirt path to the lake. While I swam, he caught minnows near the shore. When I went into the arts and crafts building, he slept in the grass outside the door until I was done. We hiked the nature trails together, listening for birds. Sometimes we'd sit in the soft moss, my back against a rock, and I'd pour out my dreams and concerns. My father had stayed back home, and I'd heard my parents talk about divorce. What was going to happen? How would my life change? Happy cocked his head listening, as if he understood. I wasn't sure of the future, but with Happy I'd be able to face whatever came my way. Having him by my side was comforting. He looked at me with his deep brown eyes like he was trying to tell me something. I think I knew; it was that he would always be there for me. I felt the same way too.

One Saturday morning my father arrived for a visit, which was unusual. He stood awkwardly in our little cabin, saying that there'd been some burglaries in the neighborhood, and that he wanted to take Happy home to protect the house.

"No!" I cried. "You can't!" I spun away from my father and pushed out the door, letting the screen slam behind me. Outside, I looked around for Happy. He wasn't there waiting for me like usual. Where could he be, when I needed him so much? He was always able to comfort me when I was upset. Now, he was nowhere to be found.

I looked behind the dining hall and the recreation center. No Happy. He wasn't by the lake, either. Without my constant companion, I felt more alone than ever. Walking the nature trail, I called his name, hoping to hear the jingle of the tags on his collar. Nothing. I curled up on a bed of soft moss and choked back tears.

After a while, I knew my mom would be getting worried. I trudged back to our cabin. Mom and Dad were there talking alongside Dad's blue sedan. My heart sank. Had they found Happy? Was my dog there in the car, about to be taken away from me? I peered in the car's windows.

Happy wasn't there!

"I can't wait any longer," Dad said. "I have to get home."

Mom sighed. "I don't understand. He always comes when called." She turned to me. "Peggy, you try."

"Happy," I called weakly, wishing with all my might that this time, just this once, he wouldn't obey. "Here boy!"

Nothing.

"Well," Dad sighed, "I guess that's that." He climbed into the driver's seat, closed the door, and pulled away. Mom and I just stood there as the late afternoon sun cast long shadows around us.

The car's wheels kicked up great clouds of dirt as it disappeared down the driveway. As the dust settled, I heard a familiar jingle. There, from around the corner, Happy came casually trotting. He sat right in front of me and looked into my eyes, almost smiling. Mom glanced at me, raising an eyebrow, as if I'd had something to do with it. Of course, I hadn't. Somehow, Happy knew all on his own that he was supposed to stay with me. I shrugged lightly, turned away, and skipped off down the path, Happy right at my heels.

I never knew what circumstances Happy had endured before he came into my life. One thing was always clear to me: No amount of hurt, or abuse, or abandonment was able to change his nature. He was as true a friend to me as he ever could be. That was just his way, and I could depend on that as long as we were together.

Devotion, or a deep emotional attachment to others, is a remarkable characteristic. It's offered even when there's little apparent value to the giver, exists through hardship and struggles, and often involves sacrifice and selflessness. Are animals capable of such a complex emotion?

In the natural world, there are hardly more perfect examples of devotion than dogs. Skeptics claim that dogs are loyal only because we give them shelter and fill their dinner bowls—dogs are devoted because they get something out of it. But dogs have genetically inherited the trait of devotion from their ancestors. In order to survive, wolves learned to hunt in packs. If they weren't devoted to others—working together for the good of the group—they all would fail. Wolves recognize which wolf is the boss, understand the roles of each member, accept their own place, and defer to the leader. Devotion keeps the entire pack strong.

In a February 2013 article in *Psychology Today*, Dr. Stanley Coren, PhD, Professor Emeritus at the University of British Columbia and author of many books on dogs, explored whether dogs have the ability to form true friendships with other dogs. He explained that dogs no longer behave precisely like wolves. While the social structure of wolves is more like cooperative social interactions, Coren wrote, "In the thousands of years since humans first domesticated dogs, we have genetically manipulated them to socialize easily and to show friendliness almost indiscriminately."[1]

An animal's capacity for devotion can be seen in both domestic and wild animals. Wolves, beavers, swans, and gibbons are devoted to their partners, mating for life. Elephants show devotion by greeting each other joyfully, caring for youngsters in the herd, warning other elephants headed for danger, and mourning deceased members of the group. One elephant even showed great devotion for her new playmate—although this was not another elephant.

TARRA'S BEST FRIEND

When it comes to selecting companions, animals generally hang around others of the same species. Perhaps it is the close proximity that draws them together, or common interests and activities. In some cases, the connection is undefinable. A mysterious attraction led Tarra the elephant to her best friend.

Tarra was a female Asian elephant who lived in The Elephant Sanctuary in Hohenwald, Tennessee. The sanctuary wasn't short of pachyderm playmates, but Tarra wasn't interested in any of them. When a stray dog wandered onto the property, Tarra made her choice. The dog clearly wasn't her size. The dog most likely had a very different past experience. Yet, Tarra wanted to be best friends forever.

Sanctuary workers named the stray dog Bella. Every day Tarra and Bella walked through the grassy park, side by side. Other stray dogs in the sanctuary avoided the elephants. Bella, however, returned Tarra's affections. They ate their meals together and swam alongside each other in the pond. Bella trusted her new best friend so much that she ran underneath Tarra's mammoth body and slept in her shade. Bella even let Tarra pat her with her huge foot!

The two animals spent every moment together, until one day Bella suffered a spinal injury. Tarra watched as the yellow dog was carried into the park's veterinary clinic for treatment. She'd need to be monitored and kept still so that she wouldn't do further damage to her spine.

That day, the elephant stood and waited outside by the gate. Then the next. And the next. For three weeks, every day, Tarra stood by the gate waiting for Bella.

At last, the sanctuary employees couldn't keep the friends apart any longer. Carefully, they carried Bella out onto the balcony. When Tarra saw Bella, she danced and stretched her trunk out toward her friend. Later, as Bella grew stronger, workers carried her outside and laid her by the gate. Tarra pushed her trunk through the rails and gently touched her friend.

There is only one word to explain the actions of the elephant who had the freedom to wander the whole sanctuary but preferred to stay close to her best friend until they could be together again: devotion. When Bella fully recovered, the friends picked up where they left off, and spent many more happy days together.

Animals are, of course, often devoted to humans as much as they are to each other. These bonds can be intense and lifelong.

ONE HUNDRED POUNDS OF LOVE

Beau loved everyone. But most of all, Leslie.

The yellow Lab puppy was just eight weeks old when he came to live with Leslie Olyott. She had his name picked out before he came home, and a blanket in a box by her bed, ready for his first night away from his mom. That night, when he whimpered, she dropped her arm over the side of the bed, and he drifted off to sleep, snuggled against her hand.

Beau loved people and animals. He played gently with Frodo the cat, and once faithfully guarded an orphaned bunny under the English Ivy. But his favorite place to be was at Leslie's heels or on her lap. Even as a full-grown, burly, lumbering dog, he still thought he belonged on her lap.

One time Leslie and her husband threw a housewarming party in their backyard. Beau soaked up all the attention from the guests—ear scratches, belly rubs, everything a Lab enjoys most. Then Leslie walked around the corner. Suddenly the guests no longer mattered. Beau bolted to his feet and sprinted toward her. One hundred pounds of love came barreling her way. He rammed into people and knocked over a table, but that didn't slow him down. When he saw Leslie, his whole world lit up. She grinned and threw out her arms to embrace him as he dashed toward her, headfirst.

Beau and Leslie enjoyed wandering the acres of woods and fields near where they lived. Beau always looked back over his shoulder as he walked, unable to bear having her out of his sight. They'd take long hikes, too, in New Hampshire's White Mountains. Beau would end up doing the trails two or three times, because he'd run up ahead, then double back to check in with Leslie, then romp off again at his boisterous pace.

On one hike, they came upon a fire tower at the top of the mountain—more like a tall platform atop a nearly impossibly-steep ladder. Leslie wanted to climb the tower, knowing she'd be rewarded with a spectacular view. "You wait here," she told Beau, patting him behind his ears, the way he liked. "I'll be back soon."

She started up the tower, carefully watching her footing. The narrow slats were open between steps, and one slip could be disastrous. About halfway up, Leslie heard people below screaming. Was someone in trouble?

"Your dog!" they yelled. "Look out! Your dog!"

She turned and looked, and there was Beau, scaling the steep wooden ladder, trying to get to her, a silly grin on his face. "I can do it, Mom!" he seemed to say.

"Oh, Beau!" She backed her way down. It took two men to help her lower the heavy dog. She never got to see the view from the top of the tower, but that didn't matter. It was more than enough that she had a dog so devoted that he'd scaled great heights to get to her.

A few summers later, Leslie took an excursion to Maine. She and Beau hiked together all day then pitched a tent for the evening. That night the temperatures dropped and the clouds burst open. Rain dripped in through the leaky tent. Beau snuggled up tight against Leslie. As she lay there in the tent, shivering, exhausted, Beau's body heat spread across her. Instead of thinking about the miserable damp conditions, all she could think about was Beau, and how devoted he'd always been. How she never had to teach him to "come," because he was always there. How he'd put his chin on her bed every morning and stare at her until she woke up, and how, when she was sick, he stayed at her side until she felt better. How he'd once protected her from a stranger in the dark. She'd never have had the confidence to make it on her own, or move away from home, or do any of the hundreds of things she would have been afraid to do, if it hadn't been for Beau by her side.

The thoughts kept her warm throughout the cold, stormy night.

A pet's determination to return home after having been separated from its family demonstrates profound devotion. For example, in the 1920s, a collie named Bobbie was lost in Indiana during a family vacation. After an extensive search, the family gave up hope and returned home without their beloved pet. They could barely believe their eyes when, six months later, Bobbie showed up at their doorstep—in Oregon! The faithful collie had traveled thousands of miles to reunite with his family.

How do animals navigate such distances? Dogs most likely rely on their keen sense of smell, which can even lead them to destinations they've never before traveled. One dog covered a much shorter distance than the famous Bobbie; however, his loyalty to his human friend was equally strong.

IN SICKNESS AND IN HEALTH

Zander the husky adored the man who'd rescued him. Maybe it was because John Dolan had found the beautiful white dog with the piercing blue eyes, scared and hungry, in the shelter. Maybe it was because John took him for long walks on the beach and playful romps at the dog park. Even though there were two other dogs in the family, Zander preferred the company of his best friend, John. Whatever the reason, Zander would do anything for John.

One day John was admitted to the Good Samaritan Hospital Medical Center to recover from a minor illness. At home, Zander was distraught. He moped around the house and stared sadly out the window. John's wife, Priscilla, could do nothing to console the pooch.

Then one morning, two days after he'd arrived in the hospital, John's cell phone rang. It was 5:45 AM. Who could be calling so early?

"Hello, who is this?" he asked.

"I work at Good Sam and I found your dog."

"What do you mean?" John asked, scratching his head.

"I found him outside the hospital. I called the number on the tags. I need you to pick him up or I'll be late for work. I'm a doctor here."

"I can't," John replied. "I'm in the hospital. I'm a patient here!"

The doctor agreed to hold the dog until Priscilla could arrive.

Later, John pieced together what must have happened. One of the family's dogs, a little red husky named Sheba, was very smart and had learned how to jump up against the door and pull down on the handle, thus opening the door. This wasn't usually a problem, because the yard was fenced. But Sheba must have opened the door early that morning, and Zander took the opportunity to run out and jump over the four-foot fence. His senses led him across a stream and down a major highway, all alone in the dark. He navigated through the woods and along paths and roads he'd never traveled before. How could he have known where he was going? How could he have known where John was sleeping?

Zander's devotion, however, somehow led him to exactly the right place. When he arrived at the hospital, he sensed that his owner was nearby and simply sat down to wait.

A few days later, John was released from the hospital and he and his dog were reunited. Zander jumped up, his furry white paws around John's waist. And John tightly hugged the dog who would go to any lengths to be beside his best friend.

———

Humans can be devoted to animals as much as it is the other way around.

The devotion that has led many pets to reunite with their families is also felt by humans separated from their pets. Leland Dirks wrote of a dog's devotion in his popular book, *Angelo's Journey*.[2] Leland's devotion in waiting at home for his real-life lost dog, however, is the rest of the story.

WAITING FOR ANGELO

One winter day, Leland's border collie disappeared, just as mysteriously as he had appeared.

Leland lives off the grid in a house he'd built in a remote area near the border between Colorado and New Mexico. A self-proclaimed hermit, his only connection to the outside world is satellite Internet. His electricity comes from the sun, and his heat from a wood fire.

One morning, as the light grew in the east, Leland saw the outline of a dog through a window. He went out to meet the canine visitor. The dog followed him everywhere. There was something special and wise about the stray. Leland's own dog had recently been killed by a hit and run driver. The mysterious dog picked up all of the other dog's toys and one-by-one placed them on her grave—One by one, fetching sticks, bones, and tennis balls.

No one in town had heard of this dog. Posters at the grocery store brought no response. And so Leland decided to keep the extraordinary dog. He named him Angelo, his angel dog.

Angelo was smart and loyal. Every day the two walked together. They explored mesas and arroyos and forests and trails. Most days, even in winter, they walked five or ten miles. They saw silly chipmunks and wise ravens, and Angelo saved Leland from disturbing a rattlesnake more than a couple of times. For four years, Angelo and Leland were best friends.

Then came the heartbreaking day when Angelo disappeared. Leland and Angelo had been walking early that morning. Angelo was prancing ahead in the new-fallen snow. He stopped and turned back to look at Leland. He barked once, sniffed the air, and ran as only a border collie can run into the distance.

"Angelo!" Leland hollered. What had he seen? Was he chasing something? He tried to run after the dog, and then tried to follow the trail of his paw prints.

Leland searched for the dog, walking for miles. When night came, he walked with a flashlight, hoping to catch some movement, to hear some howl that he might recognize. Soon it was too cold to continue walking. He returned to his house, and curled up on the floor by the door, in case the dog would scratch there in the middle of the night.

The next day he searched again. He put up posters. He notified the few neighbors that he had. He could talk of nothing else to people. "Angelo, where are you?" he wondered. Day after day, he continued to hope.

Weeks went by. Leland walked every trail that the two had walked over the four years. He lost weight, because of all the walking, and because he couldn't bring himself to eat.

Leland prayed. He was no stranger to prayer, but he prayed more and longer than he ever had in his life. He prayed first for Angelo's return. As the absence grew, he prayed for Angelo's safety and happiness, even if he couldn't return. Still later, he prayed that the dog had found a new family that needed him and would appreciate him.

"You need to get another dog. Angelo wouldn't want you to be lonely," a friend told him.

Leland closed his eyes and tried to make up his mind. He could sense, could *feel* that Angelo was still alive. He had to believe. But he also longed for the companionship of a dog that he knew would be healing. He visited an animal shelter and was rescued by a little black Labrador puppy he named Maggie. Together they would wait for Angelo's return.

Maggie walked with him on his searches for Angelo. When the puppy tired, he carried her in his arms. She slept with him on the floor, by the door, waiting for the scratch of a dog that she didn't know, except for the scent he had left all over that house in the middle of nowhere.

For forty days and forty nights, Leland never stopped searching for Angelo.

And then, one day, a delivery man stopped by with a package. As Leland signed, the driver asked, "Don't you have a dog?"

"Yes, but he's missing and..."

"No. He's not far away," the driver interrupted. "One of the other drivers saw him!"

Leland's heart raced as he peppered the man with questions. After a series of phone calls, he got directions to where a black-and-white dog who looked like Angelo had been spotted.

Leland raced to the outskirts of a small community about twenty-five miles away. And there, with dirty fur, a weary smile, and an ear nearly ripped off, sat Angelo. Leland dashed to his side. Angelo jumped up and kissed Leland's face joyfully.

"I knew I'd find you," Leland said. "I never gave up on you."

He never knew why Angelo ran off, or where Angelo had been for forty days. But he got back his angel dog. And now, when someone asks Leland if there's any point in praying, he merely nods at the dog at his side, and answers with one word: "Yes."

Bill Berloni is a renowned trainer of performing animals. Bill is the first animal trainer to win a Tony Honor for Excellence in Theater in 2011, as well as scores of other awards. The first dog he ever trained for a show was a terrier mix whom he'd rescued from a Connecticut shelter on the day the dog was to be euthanized. The show the dog performed in was *Annie*, and he went on to the original World Premier on Broadway, where he played Sandy without missing a performance for seven years. Bill has also trained the animal actors for most of the Broadway shows since 1977, including *The Wizard of Oz*, *Legally Blonde*, *Oliver*, and *Camelot*. In addition to training animals for shows, he is most devoted to helping homeless animals. All of the animals he uses in his shows come from shelters.

 RESCUED STARS

Amid the glamour and glitz of the New York City Hilton stood a big, barrel-chested New York City pit bull-mix. Harriet was destined to be a star. There was a time, however, when Bill wasn't sure that the dog stood a chance at the life she deserved.

Harriet had been abandoned and was found wandering the city streets, frightened and hungry. She had perky little ears that flopped over at the top, a big thick skull and crazy black and brown brindled fur. She was young—maybe a year old, but big—about 70 pounds. Bill looked into her deep, brown eyes. He saw her possibilities, not limitations.

When she arrived at the Humane Society of New York, where Bill works as the Director of Animal Behavior, she nuzzled up with the younger puppies, watching over them like a mother. She may have looked like a brute, but her loveable soul shined through her muscular exterior. Usually dogs come to the shelter with problems, and Bill worked to rehabilitate them. But Harriet had no issues! He felt certain she'd get adopted right away.

As you can imagine, in all of New York City, there are hundreds of needy dogs. But there are only 23 kennels in the shelter. The dogs stayed until they found a home. That's why he worked so hard understanding the individual dogs and matching people with dogs to fit their lifestyles, so they wouldn't give them up again. *Forever homes.*

Facing those sad, lonely faces in the cages always tore him up. And Harriet hurt the most. Despite her sweet nature, she was never adopted. She remained in a cage month after month. She was well-taken-care-of—plenty of love and attention and breaks to go outside for walks and play. Still, Bill worried he'd doomed Harriet to a life of confinement. Nearly every day for two years he thought of her, pouring over applications, strengthening his efforts to find her the right home.

Then Bill was asked to cast eight dogs in an upcoming Broadway musical, *Chitty Chitty Bang Bang*. After finding Sandy, Bill had promised himself that every dog he used for a show would be a rescue. He knew exactly which dog deserved one of the parts.

Most of the dogs he selected for shows couldn't win a beauty contest, but that didn't matter to Bill. He was more interested in finding dogs with a good temperament and an eagerness to please. Harriet fit the bill. At last it was time to go on stage and meet the eager rescue dogs who had arrived to try out for other roles in the show. Bill would introduce Harriet to the press at the end of the event.

They took the elevator upstairs to the Gallery, a big open exhibition room where crowds of media were gathered. Harriet remained calm despite the noise and excitement. She gazed up at Bill for direction as she walked by his side. The thumping of her tail pleaded to get on with the adventure. She was so willing!

Shelter dogs from across the city lined up to audition. The show called for a pack of dogs to run onto the stage amid lots of commotion, jump up on an actor (without hurting him or killing each other over the treats hidden in his pockets) and then at the right moment return to Bill in the darkness offstage. Bill rolled them over, scratched their bellies, and gave them cookies. He watched them play with the actor who would be swarmed by the dogs in *Chitty Chitty Bang Bang*. If the dogs weren't having a good time, he knew acting in a show wasn't right for them.

Soon it was time to introduce Harriet to the press. She trotted out, herding a group of smaller dogs, nurturing them, just as he'd observed her do in the shelter. She had a star's charisma, a presence that commanded attention. As he introduced her, he welled with emotion, happy that she was out of confinement. All these years he'd devotedly cared for her, searching for a home, and now she was going to be a star. When she was done acting, she'd have a forever home on his farm. She was hope for all the dogs ever abandoned who finally got a chance for the future.

The love and devotion offered by animals inspires us to treat them with devotion in return. Many people will remember when, in 2005, there were some who refused to evacuate New Orleans during Hurricane Katrina because they wouldn't leave behind their pets. During the 2013 flooding in Colorado, rescuers took a lesson from Katrina and were determined not to let the same thing happen. With a "No Pets Left Behind" motto, the National Guard Air Search and Rescue Operations made space for animals in helicopters, and ferried more than 800 animals to safety. Firefighters carried families, including pets, across flooded rivers via zip lines. The Red Cross provided fresh drinking water for pets and located vacancies in pet-friendly hotels. Humane Societies joined in to make arrangements for displaced pets. More lives were saved because families were willing to evacuate, knowing their loyal pets would be safe along with them.

I never had to face being separated from my pets—the day my father came to try to take away Happy came the closest. Happy always stuck by my side after school, when I walked to my best friend's house. At that time there were no leash laws where I lived, and most neighborhood dogs spent their days outside. One afternoon I went inside my friend's house to play, and Happy waited on the doorstep.

That day, while I was inside playing, the skies turned dark and a storm gathered. Happy, I knew, was afraid of thunder. Whenever a storm approached, Happy would find his way upstairs to a bedroom and squeeze under the bed or hide in a closet. Sometimes I crept in there and sat with him, stroking his neck. When the thunder boomed, he'd jump. As the storm wore on, and I remained staunchly patting him, his muscles would relax until finally another loud crash resounded and he just sunk into my side a little, trusting that I'd keep him safe. Although the thunder crashed outside that day as I played, inside with my friend I didn't give the weather a thought.

When it was time to go home, I stepped outside. There was Happy, shivering on the doorstep. He hadn't moved. Nothing had coerced him to abandon me, not even the thunder he feared so much. I hugged him close, hurting that he'd endured the storm without me there to pat his neck. I was warmed by his loyalty, that I could depend on him totally and without fail.

A popular hymn exults how God doesn't change or fail us, and how that dependability provides a "strength for today and bright hope for tomorrow."[3] That's the kind of power that devotion brings.

The LORD himself goes before you and will be with you;
he will never leave you nor forsake you.
DEUTERONOMY 31:8

CHAPTER 2
PROTECTION

Someone to watch over me

Wherever I went, Happy went too. We especially enjoyed summers at camp, where we wandered dirt paths together, his long hound ears flapping as he walked. The year I turned eight, a camp counselor named Annie visited our cabin. The front room of the cabin housed the infirmary where my mom treated cuts, scrapes, and stomachaches. "Can I get some supplies for our sleep-out tonight?" Annie asked.

While my mom packed a first aid kit, Annie turned to me. "Peggy, do you want to join us?"

I didn't answer at first. I was excited to go camping with the big kids, but also a little afraid. I hadn't spent many nights apart from my mother. What if there were wild animals, like bears and wolves? And what about the stories some of the counselors told around the campfire—could it be true that Thumper, a huge, wooden-legged man, really plucked campers right out of their sleeping bags at night?

"Can Happy come, too?" I asked at last.

"Sure," Annie laughed. "Good to have a big, strong dog for protection."

I packed my flashlight, rolled my sleeping bag, and set off with the other campers on a hike into the woods. Happy trotted along beside me, sniffing at dandelions and fiddlehead ferns. I didn't worry, with him by my side.

After setting up camp, we roasted hot dogs over the fire. Happy begged for his share, then sat by the path to keep watch. Every once in a while his ears perked at a strange squawk or hoot in the trees. Finally, we settled into our sleeping bags. The inky sky was sprinkled with millions of stars, and I felt so small. Just one quiet woof reminded me that I was safe, with Happy watching over me.

Late in the night, I was awakened by Happy's throaty growl. I sat up, pulling my sleeping bag around my shoulders.

There was a scurrying, followed by a crash.

"What is it?" I asked Annie.

"I don't know," she replied. "Happy will take care of it."

Then came a horrible odor.

"Skunk!" Annie cried.

The others woke up and shrieked, "Skunk! Skunk!"

And where was our watchdog?

He raced back to us, faster than a hungry camper responding to the dinner bell, tail between his legs. Annie shined her flashlight. The bold skunk stood there, as if mocking us. Happy hadn't run him off at all. Instead, the skunk got the best of our protector.

My terrified hound sat at my feet, rubbing his nose with his paws. His body trembled, and he cried like a baby. The way he ran back to me, shaking and whining, made me feel as if he needed someone to watch over him, too. It made me feel grown up, that he would come to me.

He rolled on the ground right in front of my sleeping bag. The odor was overwhelming. "I'm going to take him back and wash him up," I said.

"We can't stay here. We're going back, too." Annie instructed all the campers to get up and pack their gear. She cast her gaze at my pathetic pooch. "I guess he isn't much of a guard dog," she said.

"No," I said, "but he did his best." I walked right beside Happy, despite the smell. I figured at a time like this, he needed a little protecting, too. That's just what best friends do.

Best friendships are also found among animals, sometimes between unusual pairs—a cat snuggles with a bird; a retriever romps with a deer; a husky plays with a polar bear. A deer in Buffalo, New York, was determined to be a companion and protector for his special friend.

LOVE YOU DEER-LY

One warm spring day a young, male deer wandered into a cemetery in the middle of the downtown area of a large city. There were no woods surrounding the cemetery, only highways and buildings. How the deer got there, no one knew.

As he poked around, looking for good things to eat, he must have been surprised at the sound of scratching coming from a standing urn next to one of the headstones. When he peeked into the urn, there, puffed out on her nest, sat a beautiful brown goose with a sleek, black neck and white markings. She stared at him without fear or aggression. Maybe something in her eyes told the deer that the goose needed a friend. He lay down in the grass beside the urn.

A caretaker noticed the pair. "You've got to go see," he told the Forest Lawn Cemetery president, Joseph Dispenza. The caretaker's eyes grew wide as he described what he'd seen. "When I approached, the deer rose to his feet and moved in between me and the urn, like he was protecting her. He wasn't going to let me get near that goose."

Deer and geese aren't naturally enemies; however, they don't normally hang around together, either. The young deer may have been simply curious at first. Something else had made him stay.

Joseph drove to the spot near the center of the property and eagerly walked toward the headstone. He appreciated all God's creation, especially his beautiful creatures—including the two who now inhabited the cemetery's sacred acres. He watched from a distance, in awe at the unlikely pair. The deer's ears perked up, sensing someone there. Sometimes he looked around, as if alert for dogs or other animals. He was clearly protecting the female goose and her nest.

Joseph knew that geese usually parented in pairs, with the female goose sitting on the eggs and the male goose standing guard to protect the nest. It seemed as though the goose had lost her mate. The young deer stepped in to keep watch over her and the nest. As Joseph took in the beautiful scene, he felt he was witnessing an act of pure, unexpected benevolence. He warmed with the beautiful lesson he felt settling around him. There was no other way to explain it. "This is truly a divine message, delivered in a most unusual way so we could learn from it," he said later. "A modern parable, if you will. We need to be kind to each other. To look out for each other."

Why did the deer do it? What did he have to gain?

"It's one creature of the Lord looking out after another creature of the Lord," he said. A lesson for us all.

In the following story, once again we see animals protecting humans. Since we share our lives with animals, they consider us part of their pack and will often protect us from predators, too.

GUARDIAN ANGEL CALF

A narrow dirt path stretched between the front yard and the back field of the Rocky Ridge Refuge in Arkansas. Janice Wolf picked her way along the bumpy ground beside a large pile of rocks. Her llama was ahead on the path, and her Watusi calf, Lurch, plodded along near her side.

The fall air felt crisp as she took a shallow breath. She'd just gotten out of the hospital the day before after a procedure on her lungs. She wanted to check on the animals before going back inside her home to rest.

Without warning, the llama stopped, then veered off to the side. "Now what on earth could have caused such odd behavior?" she wondered. Distracted watching the llama who was skittering off over the rocks, she bumped into Lurch, who had also stopped on the path. "Get a move on," she said, tapping him on the brawny shoulder.

Instead, Lurch turned sideways, blocking her from proceeding. Janice glanced at her flimsy flip-flops. Not good for trying to maneuver over the rock pile to get around him. She pushed him again, but he held firm. The only way to get by was to squeeze around in front of him. She grabbed hold of his horns to use as balance. Lurch became restless, shifting uneasily.

Just as Janice was about to step her foot down on the other side, Lurch tossed his head. The sudden jerk threw her off balance. She stumbled backward. That's when she saw the copperhead snake! It was coiled right where she had been about to step down. Horrified, she shrieked. Her dogs came running over to the fence to see what was wrong, and she shooed them away.

When she looked back, there was the snake lying limp in the dirt. Lurch had stomped the snake to death.

While copperhead bites aren't usually fatal to adults, for Janice it very likely would have been, due to her weakened condition from her recent hospitalization. Thanks to the insistent actions of her Watusi calf, she'd been protected from harm.

And then there is the story of two stealthy dogs, Agatha and Christie, who investigated a mysterious noise in their home and took the matter into their own paws.

HOME ALONE

The sun had set and the street lights in Pamela Webster's Philadelphia neighborhood brightened. Pamela and her shepherd mixes, Agatha and Christie, were just completing their nightly walk. The dogs wore special halters that reduced pulling on the leash and fit securely around their snouts.

They walked up the front steps to the house and Pamela unlocked the door. Her husband was attending school and often stayed late to work on projects, so she and the dogs were frequently home alone at night.

As she stepped into the hall, Agatha and Christie immediately pulled away, dashed into the pitch-dark dining room and barked furiously. This was not their usual run-of-the-mill bark. There was a definite urgency, a warning in their tone that told her something was wrong.

"Come here! Come back here!" she called.

The dogs continued barking.

She pulled out treats that she carried in her coat pocket. "Want a biscuit?" Still nothing. No matter how much she called or tried to coax them, the normally obedient dogs wouldn't return to her.

She had no idea what her dogs were barking at, but she couldn't turn on the light without walking through the dining room, and her senses told her that wasn't a good idea. She didn't have a phone with her, either. Amid the dogs barking, she heard whispers and feet scuffling. The dogs had someone cornered in the dining room.

"I'm going to take my dogs and we're going outside," she called into the dark. "You'll have two minutes to get out of the house before I come back with the dogs—*without* their muzzles." She hoped this little deception would work. The dogs could very well bite through their special harnesses, but apparently had chosen not to.

Using her firmest voice, she somehow got Agatha and Christie to return to her. They stepped out front, and after the promised two minutes, went back inside.

The intruders were gone.

Pamela later discovered that the would-be burglars had entered through an access hatch in the roof. If her dogs hadn't been with her that evening, she'd have walked unprotected into a dangerous situation. Thanks to Agatha and Christie she was home safe and sound.

Even animals in zoos have been observed demonstrating protective behavior towards humans. The actions of a male silverback gorilla at the Jersey Zoo shocked everyone when a little boy fell into the gorilla enclosure.

GENTLE GIANT

One warm August day the Jersey Zoo was crowded with visitors, fascinated by the massive, intimidating creatures in the gorilla complex. Jambo, the lead silverback, sat sedately, clearly in charge. He glanced up at the crowd, at times studying the faces, at times turning his back and showing little interest.

Up above, a father lifted his little boy atop the tall barrier so the boy could get a better look. In an instant, the boy slipped and, horrifically, plunged twelve feet down into the enclosure. The boy lay motionless in the cement trench at the base of the wall, blood pooling around his head.

All around, people were screaming and crying. Jambo startled at the commotion. He looked at the boy, then back at his troop. The gorillas were usually peaceful unless challenged or disturbed. As leader of his troop, Jambo sensed that some of the younger males were uneasy with the boy's presence. That could be dangerous. A female gorilla and her baby approached. Jambo darted over and stood between her and the boy. *Don't touch*, his body language said. They backed away.

Jambo sat a few feet away from the injured boy, who was unconscious. He sniffed the child's head, picking up information as he would in the wild. The zoo visitors screamed. "We should throw rocks at him and scare him away!" someone shouted. Fortunately, they were dissuaded from that action. An angry gorilla would certainly be dangerous. No one could predict what the gorilla would do. Even the keepers didn't walk around inside the enclosure and interact with the gorillas. Everyone worried that Jambo would harm the helpless boy.

Then Jambo did something no one expected. He reached out and very gently rubbed the boy's back. He looked at him as if concerned. Several times, other gorillas tried to get closer. Jambo had only to stare at them to keep them at bay. The crowd quieted, amazed. The fearsome gorilla, so huge and powerful, was actually protecting the injured boy.

When the boy finally awoke, he began to cry. The wails unsettled Jambo—he wasn't used to such a sound in his enclosure. The wise leader turned and signaled for the troop to follow him. As they moved to the enclosure, zookeepers rushed to usher them into their quarters where they could be kept secure.

As soon as it was clear, zookeepers and medical personnel jumped over the barrier. The boy had a fractured skull and broken arm and leg, but he recovered from his injuries. Jambo had done his part by keeping the boy safe from the rest of the troop. Although massive and powerful, because of his heroism at the zoo, Jambo became known as the Gentle Giant.

Some dangers in life affect both humans and animals, and they go unnoticed until a watchful pet alerts the family of an impending disaster.

One cat in Colorado yowled and batted at her sleeping family, until they awoke and took note of rapidly rising river waters outside. Minutes after they evacuated, their home was swept away in a flood. Another cat alerted his family to a carbon monoxide leak. One dog barked to awaken his family when a fire erupted in the kitchen. These vigilant pets most likely saved their families' lives.

Courageous working dogs are specially trained to help keep us safe. They patrol with police, search for weapons at airports and train stations, serve in the military, and sniff out drugs, weapons, and explosives. After terrorist bombs tragically killed three and maimed more than 200 spectators at the 2013 Boston Marathon, bomb-sniffing dogs have been increasingly visible at public events. In 2014, the Napa Valley Marathon employed four specially trained bomb-detecting dogs. The race went off without incident, and the dogs created a calming effect on the runners and spectators.

For all they do to keep us safe, we have a responsibility to guard and defend our animals, as well. In 1866, an organization was formed to help protect animals. The American Society for the Prevention of Cruelty to Animals (ASPCA) works nationally to rescue animals from abuse, lobby for humane laws, and share resources with shelters across the country. Two of their major projects are rescuing animals from puppy mills—large-scale breeding operations with overcrowded and unsanitary conditions—and investigating and raiding dog-fighting operations. They also protect animals from hoarding situations, or instances when someone houses a large number of animals without properly providing adequate shelter, nutrition, sanitation, and veterinary care. The ASPCA is a valuable organization to keep animals safe, bring abusers to trial, and educate the public.

In some other parts of the world, animals are less fortunate than they are in the United States. Molly Mednikow saw a need in one such place, and set out to find a solution.

TOO MANY STREET DOGS

Molly crouched to pat the little dog, so dirty there was no way to tell what color he really was underneath. He was rail thin, his scrawny legs barely carrying him along the dusty road. He most likely hadn't had a home, or veterinary care, or attention his whole life. That's the way it was in this community on the Amazon, so poor that the people struggled to simply survive.

She cradled the weak pup and carried him to the rickshaw. She'd save this dog. But then, she thought, there were so many more.

Molly was visiting the remote region of Iquitos, Peru. She found beauty in the land and the people. She found sorrow in the large number of street dogs who roamed around. When she returned home to Georgia, she couldn't get those dogs out of her mind. Even when she closed her eyes at night and tried to sleep, the images wouldn't go away.

In 2004 she returned for another visit to the country. She stayed in a hotel, where employees shooed away dogs outside the building. She, however, kept food on hand to feed the street dogs who approached her cautiously.

One evening when she returned to the hotel, she saw two mangy, malnourished dogs waiting for her at the front entrance. The attendants hadn't yet chased them away. Molly waited until no one was looking, and she snuck the ailing dogs into her room.

That night she eased them into the hotel bathtub and washed away the mud and fleas. The dogs probably had never felt the soothing comfort of being clean. "You're safe. You're safe," she repeated. She watched over them until finally they relaxed. But she didn't get a wink of sleep that night.

Early in the morning she snuck the dogs back out of the hotel and brought them to a local veterinarian's office. The vet had been kind. He'd helped her many times before, but he was running out of space. He couldn't keep all the sick, abandoned, desperate dogs she found.

Molly had no choice. She never boarded the plane back to Georgia. She made a bold decision. She sold her share of a family jewelry business, rented space, and built kennels and an exam room. Most people thought she'd lost her mind. Nothing else, however, seemed as important as caring for those innocent dogs who didn't have a chance. That year she started the organization Amazon Community Animal Rescue, Education and Safety (CARES). They offer neutering to help control the street dog population, find homes, and provide food and medical attention in the only no-kill dog shelter in Peru's Amazon River Basin.

One year, a dog named Calipso came to stay at the Amazon CARES shelter. Calipso had lived on the streets for many years, usually hanging out near the local Western Union office, where the proprietor fed her table scraps. No one knew how she got her name, but it was a boy's name. Imagine everyone's surprise when Calipso became pregnant. Her long shaggy coat and her tendency to hide in dark corners had hidden her gender.

Calipso had a miserable life. The townspeople threw mud and rocks at her and kicked her out of the way. Pet ownership in the Amazon is quite different from that in the United States. Pets are not pampered. Very few have collars or identification. Most dogs are free-roaming, without anyone to care for them. Her teeth were mere nubs due to years of scraping food off of concrete walkways. After years of living on the streets, lacking security and affection, she was fearful and shy. Molly rubbed her ears. "You're safe here," she said.

Calipso bore a litter of seven puppies, but day by day, each puppy failed to survive—a common event when pregnant dogs are malnourished. It broke Molly's heart, because Calipso was such a devoted mother.

Although she already had four house pets, Molly brought Calipso inside her home. Calipso often hid behind doors and under tables. Her other dogs happily joined Molly on top of her bed, but Calipso felt more comfortable sleeping under the bed.

Soon, her live-in household employee, Lady, fell in love with, and adopted, Calipso. The dog slept in Lady's room at night, and Molly still had the benefit of watching over her by day. Molly and Lady devoted hours a day to showering Calipso with affection, trying to bring her out of her shell. At times Molly would even force Calipso to sit on her lap so that she could stroke her fur and whisper sweet nothings in her ear.

Then one day Molly was sitting in the living room, and Calipso softly padded up and jumped into her lap. She looked into the dog's beautiful brown eyes and called her by name. Calipso's muscles softened, and she melted into Molly's embrace.

Finally, the dog had learned to trust. There in that safe environment, protected from the tropical Amazon weather, the rocks and kicks, and the pains of hunger, she had also learned to love for probably the first time in her hard life.

Molly expanded her vision to educate residents in humane, responsible pet ownership. Through Molly's compassionate determination, Amazon CARES has educated a whole culture of people to protect and cherish dogs as part of the family, and to learn to live in harmony with the beautiful animals of the Amazon region.

Janice, the Arkansas woman with the protective calf mentioned previously, runs a refuge for orphaned and injured animals. Among the many creatures she rescues are rabbits, raccoons, a zebra, donkeys, horses, water buffalo, cows, and dogs. She has written this prayer, urging people to help protect and care for God's creatures.

A PRAYER FOR DOGS

Dear Lord as we start each day
There's just one gift for which I pray.
Please watch over all dogs everywhere
And bless them with someone to care.

Watch over the pups with plenty to eat
And hungry strays out on the street
Those getting treats each time they yap
And those that struggle for every scrap.

Those that sleep on a nice soft bed
Those with hard ground under their head
Those who play with girls and boys
And those that never had any toys.

Those kept clipped and brushed and clean
And scruffy ones that don't smell too keen
Those who get to ride in cars
And those that sit behind cage bars.

Those that flunk obedience school
Dig up the yard, snore and drool
Chew up your stuff, chase the cat
And still they're loved in spite of that.

And those that are as good as gold
But left out to shiver in the cold.
Chained up and forgotten there,
They long for a warm home to share.

Please God as we end each night
Help more people do what's right.
For each dog they meet, to do their best
And send your comfort to all the rest.

Some organizations look out for endangered species and help defend wildlife from loss of habitat. Others work to protect domestic animals. One man realized that farm animals—even those destined for slaughter—deserve a voice.

HILDA'S STORY

It was a sight he'd never get used to—the dead pile. Gene Baur stood outside the stockyard in Lancaster, Pennsylvania. The blazing summer sun beat at his brow. He swiped an arm across his forehead. At his feet, the discards of factory farming—a pile of dead cows, pigs, and sheep. How could anyone be so heartless? How could innocent lives amount to this?

A few years earlier, he'd begun investigating factory farms, stockyards, and slaughterhouses. Too often, what he discovered was dreadful, neglectful conditions. Animals packed in so tightly they couldn't walk, turn around or lie down. Animals denied wholesome food and fresh air. Billions of animals exploited by the food industry needed protection. Who would be their voice, if not him? He and a partner founded Farm Sanctuary in Wilmington, Delaware. He would educate people and campaign for changes. And, most of all, protect the animals.

There was no end to the hard work. And this—the dead pile—was too much to take. He wanted nothing more than, just this once, to run from the sight, to close his eyes and hide. Then, in the pile, he saw a movement. A sheep lifted its head. His gut twisted at the horror. The sheep was alive!

Ignoring the stench, the insects, the ghastliness so great his heart could barely stand it, he climbed closer, reached in, and grabbed the sheep by her front legs. As he pulled, dead animals fell from around her. He focused only on her eyes—a spark of life inside pleaded. *Hope.* He lifted her, hurried her to his truck, and headed to the vet's. Even if there was no chance, even if she had to be euthanized, she wouldn't die like that. Not in a fetid pile on the ground in the ghastly heat outside the slaughterhouse.

The veterinarian examined the grimy, starving creature Gene laid on the table. "I don't know, Gene," he said, his voice trailing.

"Do what you can," Gene said. "Make her comfortable."

The doctor gave her fluids and antibiotics, and cleaned her wounds. The sheep lifted her head. Gene looked in her eyes. There it was again—hope. She struggled to her feet. She was standing—the poor little sheep, left for dead.

She survived. Gene named her Hilda. Hilda became the affirmation that what he was doing in Farm Sanctuary was necessary and vital. Hilda—the sheep who had been given up for dead—went on to live at Farm Sanctuary for ten more years, safe and protected, fed and cared for. Gene continues to commit his work to encouraging others to recognize farm animals as individuals, much like we do with cats and dogs, and fighting for changes in the factory farming system.

Protection may be a strong presence standing guard or a physical intervention between someone and a threatening force. My dogs, Kelly and Ike, make me feel safe when we're out on walks in the city. Who'd want to bother me when I'm making my way down the sidewalk with a spirited dog on each side? I'm also comforted by their late-night barks. Just a few weeks ago, they started raising a racket. They often bark at car doors and people coming and going in the neighborhood, so I didn't think too much of it. But then they ran to the kitchen window, which looks out over our driveway. *Strange*, I thought. Usually they bark at the front door, having heard sounds on the main road.

"I'll check it out," Mike said. He opened the front door, stepped onto the porch, and looked around. "Nothing," he reported.

The dogs quieted down.

The next morning Mike and I set out to do some errands. "It looks like the dome light's on," Mike said as we approached the car in the driveway.

When I opened the passenger side door, I noticed that the DVD monitor on the back of the seat was hanging by a wire. It couldn't have just fallen out—it was installed inside the headrest and would have had to been pried out with a tool. "Someone must have tried to break in!"

That's when we realized that the dogs' keen ears had heard the prowler in the driveway. Their barking had scared him off before he'd completed the job.

When we got home, I fluffed up their doggy pillows, hugged them tight, and promised to keep them each safe, forever.

Do not fear, for I am with you. Do not be afraid, for I am your God;
I will strengthen you. I will help you, I will uphold you with my
victorious right hand.

ISAIAH 41:10 NRSV

CHAPTER 3
ACCEPTANCE

I love you just the way you are

I was *that* kid, the one pestering their parents, always begging for pets.

In addition to cats and dogs, I kept hamsters, gerbils, goldfish, turtles, and rabbits, but my favorite small pets were my guinea pigs.

I got Gipper, my beautiful long-haired guinea pig, at the Vermont State Fair. While my friends stood in long lines for rides that twirled them around and threatened to empty their stomachs, I hung around the livestock tents. Walking past odorous stalls of cows and pens of chickens, I stopped abruptly when I came upon a cage of small pets. A handwritten sign displayed a Latin name: *Peruvian cavy*. Never before had I seen such a beautiful creature as the tri-colored guinea pig before me. Long locks cascaded, nearly covering her eyes. Instead of spending my money on candy apples and fried dough, I happily handed it all over to purchase my very own guinea pig. Ha! My best friend had only a dopey plush purple bear to show for her day, but I got to take home a real, live animal!

"Why don't you go out and play? Do you want to call a friend?" my mom would ask the rest of that summer. I never listened. I was too busy creating cardboard tunnels and hideouts for Gipper, and letting her explore outside in a patch of clover.

That fall I started seventh grade. The once-easy network of social interaction became complicated. Kids developed new interests, more sophisticated than mine. In addition, my parents were going through a divorce. After school, I retreated to my room, dropped the needle of my stereo onto a scratchy Elton John album, and gingerly lifted Gipper out of her cage. She rested happily atop a soft towel on my lap and made purring sounds as I stroked her back. No matter how confused or upset I felt, Gipper didn't pull away. She accepted me as a friend and caretaker.

Near the end of the school year, my science teacher announced that she needed someone to keep Charlie, the class guinea pig. "Anyone who wants him, write your name on a piece of paper and drop it in this bowl. Of course, you'll need your parents' permission." I just *had* to have that adorable blond critter who squeaked and scattered his cedar shavings while we sat studying photosynthesis and locating cytoplasm in cell diagrams. I scribbled my name on a piece of notebook paper—one of the few in class who confidently anticipated their parents' permission.

I could barely believe it when my name was drawn!

Although I knew Gipper accepted me, I hoped that she'd accept Charlie, too. Fortunately, they got along great. I loved watching them scamper around together as if best friends. After school, I'd tell them secrets. I'd tell them about the mean girl at school, and about how my father moved out of the house. Stroking their fur and listening to their soft squeaks always made me feel better.

One day Gipper lay in the corner of her cage, still and quiet. That night I whispered my prayers. "God, I know this is just a small animal, but you love all your creation. Please, could you help her get better?"

In the morning, I looked hopefully into the cage. Charlie was running around, knocking over the food bowl. Gipper was still quiet. Then I saw something. Something wonderful. Gipper had babies!

The tiny guinea pigs came in every size and color, with short hair, long hair, and crazy, cowlicky hair. Some had Charlie's sleek blond hair. "Mom, mom, come see!" I called. Mom ran into the room and then put her arm around me as we counted—six, seven, eight babies!

Although I wished I could keep them, when they were ready I found them all good homes. I worked hard to match them with just the right families. Hopefully, when some other girl was having a bad day, she'd know that at least one small creature was there for her. Loving her. Accepting her for who she was. And hopefully, that would be just what she needed.

Pets have a wonderful way of making people feel accepted. Cats and dogs visit senior care facilities and interact with residents who may not connect with other people. One elderly Canadian man with Alzheimer's disease spent most days in his nursing home room, rarely speaking to the other residents. When he did, he used his native language, German, and was rarely understood. One morning his wife took him down to the lobby, where they saw a big, black and white tom cat. He took one look at the cat and stopped, his eyes wide. Leaning on his cane, he bent close to the ground. The tension in his face melted away as he smiled. "Oh! *Mieze, mieze. Miezekätzchen*," he cried, which is German for "kitty cat." His wife's eyes brimmed with tears as she led him to a chair. The cat rubbed against his legs. Others may not have understood the man's language. The cat didn't mind at all. For those moments, as he stroked the cat, he felt accepted. After that, his wife brought him to visit the cat nearly every day, and he always brightened as he called out, "*Miezekätzchen!*"

The reason animals help seniors is simple. It's the same reason animals are good for any of us. They accept everyone, no matter how young or old, healthy or infirm, sharp or confused. And that feeling of acceptance provides comfort and encouragement, especially at times when life seems rocky.

A wonderfully empathetic cat once helped inspire a positive self-image for a New Jersey woman.

CAT'S EYE VIEW

Melissa Roberson stood in front of the mirror and frowned. No, she didn't expect to see a movie star staring back at her. She wasn't looking for perfection. But the reflection was discouraging. Although she tried to take care of herself, there was no getting around it—she was overweight. Every lump and wrinkle seemed magnified in the glass. "Yes, I know I have an imperfect body," she complained to the mirror. "You don't have to remind me."

The act of undressing in front of anyone had always filled her with anxiety. All her body image neuroses tumbled around in her brain. She never remembered a time when she felt good about her figure. Her cousin had been Miss Mississippi, for Pete's sake. How could she compete with that? Her family was critical of her weight, so she snuck food. Now a lifetime of emotions and bad habits had taken their toll.

She sighed and started to turn away. She felt a soft rub against her ankle. Her beautiful longhaired, gray Ragdoll cat, Chet, had walked over to say hello. He looked admiringly into the mirror. "That's easy for you," she said. "You're gorgeous." Chet rubbed against her again. He looked up adoringly. He gazed at her with his blinky eyes, sending her "cat kisses." Wait a minute—he wasn't looking at his own reflection. He was looking at her—looking at her with the same loving, admiring look as always. Chet wasn't the least bit phased that she was standing there in her birthday suit, that she was overweight, that she had varicose veins, or any of the other so-called negative aspects of a sixty-year-old body.

She reached down and scratched Chet's ears. Chet loved her, just the way she was. She would always be important and wonderful to her cat. She smiled as she put on her robe and got ready for the day. Somehow it was a little easier to be less critical of herself when she felt that no-strings-attached love. With pets, there is no judgment. That's one of the most wonderful parts of their love.

Animals don't care about our weight, appearance, or physical disabilities. Animals with their own physical challenges are especially suited to teach others to accept themselves, just the way they are.

JUST LIKE ME

The eight-year-old boy took one look at the tan and white pup and exclaimed, "He's just like me!"

Lentil the French bulldog had come to visit the boy. They met at an event where children with "facial differences" could get to know a dog with "snout differences." The boy and the dog both had a deformation of the face called cleft palate. Lentil, so named because he looked like a bean when he was a pup, was born with a serious medical condition—a double cleft nose, cleft lip, and cleft hard and soft palate. An abnormal opening in the roof of his mouth had caused the two sides of his palate to remain unfused. Luckily, a local rescue group took him in, and Lindsay Condefer became the little bean's new mom. She fed him with a tube every two to three hours, for four months. "Weigh . . . calculate . . . tube feed . . . love," Lindsay said. "That was our schedule." Later Lentil underwent surgery. Lindsay started a Facebook page to keep friends, family, and anyone who wanted an update posted about his progress. The page was surprisingly popular. Everyone fell in love with the cute little guy.

One day Lindsay received a message from a woman in Illinois. "My daughter and I follow Lentil's posts every day," the woman wrote. "It's funny that the public is so attracted to Lentil's looks," she added, "yet, he has the same condition for which my daughter has been ridiculed every day." That message hit Lindsay hard. Was there something she and Lentil could do to make a difference? She contacted the Children's Craniofacial Association to ask what she could do to help their cause. "These kids need confidence," Lindsay realized, "to be themselves and not feel judged." Lindsay and Lentil began speaking to groups at hospitals, special camps, and retreats. When the children see Lentil, they're full of questions. They're amazed when they discover what they have in common. They pose for pictures. Lentil likes to have the kids throw him his ball. The kids understand that in most ways he's just like any other pup.

Lindsay held out Lentil's toy to the young boy. "You're right, he is just like you!" she said. "Do you like to play ball? Because Lentil does, too!" The boy nodded and threw the ball, and Lentil galloped off. The boy grinned.

Lentil accepts the kids, and the kids, seeing a loving animal with a condition just like them, learn to love and accept themselves, too. "There is so much more to people than just their outward appearance," Lindsay says.

And that goes for dogs, too.

Another special dog, Frankie, helped children learn that they can do amazing things, even though they may face obstacles.

THE WALK 'N ROLL DOG

The school kids formed a circle around the little dog. "Frankie and her mom are here to tell you something special," the teacher told them. All around the miniature dachshund sat kids—tall and short, dressed in tidy striped shirts or wrinkled tees, hair done up in fancy braids or hanging shaggy around their face. Some were outgoing and popular, and some were insecure and shy. Frankie saw the kids, but of course she didn't notice all those things.

"Does anyone know why Frankie has these wheels?" her mom, Barbara Techel, asked.

"To play?" the kids guessed.

"To race?"

"To pull things?"

"Good guesses," Barbara said. "These wheels belong to Frankie's wheelchair!"

She told the kids about the horrible day when Frankie injured her spine and became paralyzed. Frankie couldn't move her back legs. Then Barbara explained how Frankie was fitted for a custom wheelchair.

"Frankie didn't know how to use her wheelchair right away. I had to teach her. I made a row of dog treats down the sidewalk. Frankie was so anxious to get the treats, she moved her front legs and rolled over to one, stopped, gobbled it up, then rolled on to the next." The children laughed, waiting in anticipation as Barbara told them how Frankie learned to walk. "Before long, I could throw a treat ahead of us and she'd run really fast to go get the treat.

"When we got to the end of our street, some little boys were playing in the park and saw Frankie. For a moment I worried they might make fun of her because she's in a wheelchair. One of the little boys came up to us and said, 'Hey, cool, your dog has tires!' I thought that was great that the boy thought Frankie's wheelchair was cool."

Then a little girl in the class frowned and said, "I feel sorry for her."

Barbara smiled gently at the schoolchildren. "Frankie doesn't want that! You see, boys and girls, Frankie's wheelchair is a tool that allows her to live the best life that she can. She can do most things all dogs do. She can go for walks. She can eat, she can sniff the grass, she can play with other dogs. And her favorite thing to do is chase squirrels!"

The children clapped for all the things Frankie could still do. A little girl with blonde hair and bright blue eyes raised her hand. "Does it hurt for Frankie to be in her wheelchair?"

"Oh no, not at all. She isn't in any pain. In fact, I don't even think she realizes she has wheels as back legs. When you look at Frankie, does she look sad or happy to you?"

"She looks happy!" the children called out.

"Yes, I agree. I believe she is happy, too. See, with her wheelchair, there's practically nothing she can't do." As if to demonstrate, Frankie raced back and forth and around the circle, her front legs trotting along, her back legs supported by the smoothly rolling wheels. "We call her the Walk 'n Roll Dog!" Barbara laughed.

The kids reached out to pat her. Frankie gave each child a special nuzzle. "The message Frankie has for all of you today," Barbara said, "is that we all have challenges—they are a part of life. When you face a challenge, you have a choice, just like Frankie does. Is it better to be positive or negative?"

The kids yelled in unison, "Positive!"

"That's right! Bravo! So when you are faced with something difficult or confusing, be positive, and you will navigate your challenge a little more easily."

"Also, I want you to know that Frankie doesn't feel sorry for herself. Remember when we said that she looks happy? She accepts her condition and wakes up eager each day." Barbara stopped for a moment, took Frankie out of her wheelchair, and held her close. "Even though Frankie's back legs don't work anymore, she's still the same Frankie she always was. Just like when something difficult happens in your life, you're still you." Holding her hand on her heart, Barbara said, "Deep down in your heart, you are always you, no matter what."

A young boy with glasses shouted, "I just got glasses and I'm still me!"

"Exactly! Your glasses, just like Frankie's wheelchair, are your tool to help you see better. And yes, you are still you even with your new glasses!"

Frankie took another spin around the circle, and the kids all laughed and clapped. Barbara grinned. "Oh, and Frankie also wants you to all keep on rolling!"

The perfect pet may be young or old, energetic or laid-back. But when a pet doesn't fit our perception of how they should behave, they're often cast aside. Understanding an animal can be the key to acceptance.

LAST CHANCE

The man was offering the small pinto pony for free. "Why would someone want to just give away a horse? Is there something wrong with him?" Catherine Madera wondered. She stroked the pinto's bony side—too thin. The horse was underfed and neglected, having been kept in a pasture all alone. His coloring, however, was striking, with bold reddish-brown and white spots, and a beautiful tri-colored mane. With a little love and attention, he could be a great horse.

What might happen to him if she didn't step in? She was his last chance, she thought. Chance. That would be his name. An experienced horsewoman, Catherine took Chance home and introduced him to the lush green pasture. He looked away. "It's okay," she said, her voice soft. "You're safe here."

The next few days she reached out to him, petting and brushing his filthy coat. He just stood there with no reaction. Catherine was used to a mutually warm and connected friendship with her horses. "Why did I get this horse?" She wondered. "He doesn't even like me." Catherine tried putting the horse into her friend's larger herd of riding horses to socialize him. They wanted nothing to do with him. *A horse not even accepted by his own kind? Maybe that's why the man was giving him away?*

She started training Chance. Maybe some consistency would help. He seemed to understand her cues, but he didn't follow through. What came easily to the other horses was difficult for Chance. When she put him under the saddle, he squirmed awkwardly. On the trail, his clumsy pace made it difficult to negotiate the terrain. "Chance, what is wrong with you?" Catherine snapped. She even prayed about him as she did her chores. "Lord, I don't know what to do. Please make him into a better horse."

One day she was in Chance's pen with her back turned. The horse reared up. "Whoa, boy!" Catherine called. Chance struck her on the shoulder with his hoof. She raced out of the stall, terrified. Why had he done that? She couldn't understand his behavior. Once he even fell while her ten-year-old daughter was riding him. Fortunately, she was okay, but that was the end of Chance as a riding horse. She couldn't risk herself, or anyone in the family, getting hurt. Catherine just couldn't take the chance on Chance.

The next morning she was in the barn as Chance dozed in his stall. His neck was bowed in a graceful arch. Catherine saw the potential for a sweet, loving horse. He always tried his best. He accepted her leadership. Still, despite her best efforts, she couldn't change his frustrating behaviors. As she turned to lift a heavy bale of hay, a huge crash sounded from the horse's stall. She rushed over and gasped. Chance lay on the floor. He'd fallen over on his side. His legs shook. She recognized that he was having a seizure.

After a blood panel and physical evaluation, the vet explained that Chance's behavioral issues were actually due to a serious neurological disorder. He'd never been fully capable of the connections Catherine had wanted. Catherine felt stabs of guilt. She had judged him for what she perceived as a lack of brains, performance, and ability.

When she returned Chance to his stall, she gave him an extra scoop of oats. "Good boy," she said, patting his neck. Given his medical condition, it was a miracle she'd been able to ride him at all. Looking back, she knew that she never should have put him in some of those training situations. Still, despite everything, Chance had tried as hard as he could. He may not have been the calmest horse, or the smartest, or even the easiest to love. Without a doubt, however, he'd taught her one of the greatest lessons: Every creature on earth deserves understanding. And by understanding Chance—all of his needs and all of his gifts—she learned to accept Chance for the horse he was and not the horse she wanted him to be. And that was good enough.

Unfortunately, many people judge animals based on traits other than their personality and nature. Animal shelter workers have documented Black Dog Syndrome—where black-colored dogs are not as readily adopted as other dogs. People don't accept black dogs because they're often portrayed in literature and movies as scary and menacing. Black dogs, of course, are just as affectionate and loyal as any other dog. The same situation is seen with black cats, who are frequently associated with witchcraft and bad luck. Animal shelters consistently have a more difficult time finding them homes.

Some animals are also unfairly judged based on their breed. When governing bodies consider certain breeds dangerous, they have enacted Breed Specific Legislation (BSL), which restricts or bans people from owning those breeds, even if the specific dog has never had an instance of aggression. Some of the dogs targeted in BSL are pit bulls, Rottweilers, German shepherds, and mastiffs. Opponents of BSL claim that these dogs are not inherently dangerous, and that problems are most often the result of abusive, irresponsible, or reckless owners. Judging animals as individuals, not by breed or color, could save many wonderful pets from homelessness or euthanasia.

An inspiring program in North Carolina strives to correct teens' misunderstandings about certain animals.

NATURE WALK DISCOVERY

In a log cabin deep in the Blue Ridge Mountains, amid acres of fields, streams, and woods, is a very special classroom. A man with a peppery beard and graying hair pulled back in a ponytail is the instructor.

One day he stood in front of the group, holding a black rat snake, his sleek body wrapped around Steve's arm.

"Is it going to bite me?" asked Jason, his long hair sweeping over his eyes.

Steve O'Neil, a naturalist at Trails Carolina, shook his head, smiling. Jason was usually quiet and withdrawn, continually in and out of trouble.

Trails Carolina is a therapeutic wilderness program for troubled boys and girls. Many of the youth deal with anxiety, trauma, or substance abuse. They may struggle in school or have behavioral issues or difficult home lives. Steve teaches science-based natural resource and wildlife conservation classes. The youth in his program often come to him with strong preconceptions that certain species of animals are mean or scary, or even evil.

"No," Steve said. "This type of snake doesn't bite. He's gentle and peaceful." Steve walked near each student, giving them a chance to examine the reptile closely. "Snakes are misunderstood, in part because they're unusual. They're different. But we need these animals in our environment. They control the rodent population. So if you see them in your garden or your yard, just let them go about their business and they will quietly and effectively work to keep your land healthy and diverse."

Trails Carolina also incorporates frogs, salamanders, lizards, insects, spiders, turtles, and opossums into their program, helping kids accept these animals as interesting, important, and even lovable creatures.

After time in the classroom, Steve took the kids outside for a nature walk; there are hundreds of acres of beautiful mountainous forest, fields, and streams to explore.

"Look! There's a snake, like you were showing us in class!" a student observed, stepping back cautiously.

Steve picked up the snake, smiling and running his hand down its smooth back. As he explained how the snake lived, and what it liked to eat, the kids relaxed. They began to see the snake as a creature with a place in the environment, not as a scary enemy.

"Okay now, who wants to hold him?" Steve asked.

Some of the kids laughed nervously. "That's okay for you to do," Jason said, "you're used to it. It's slimy and gross. No way, I don't want to touch it!"

Steve nodded thoughtfully. "How do you think it feels to be this snake, and have you fear him, and not want to be anywhere near him?"

"I can tell you *just* how it feels," Jason answered quietly. "I feel that way every day at school. The other kids think I'm bad because I don't hang around in their groups, or play their sports. They bully me and call me names. They don't know what I'm like! They don't know how I feel."

"That's right." The snake slid across Steve's hands. Its forked tongue searched the air.

Jason flinched.

"This tongue is actually a sensory organ. When it flicks out, it's collecting bits of information to tell the snake about its location, if there is any food available, and if there are any enemies around. The snake can't shoot venom, or injure people with its tongue. It's just a tool."

"I didn't know that," Jason said.

"Now would you like to hold him?"

Jason hesitated. Then he bravely took a step closer. "I guess..." He reached out a shaky hand. Steve gently transferred the snake. While Jason squirmed, he also couldn't stop grinning. He was doing something he never thought he'd dare—or want—to do.

"It's weird," he said, "but he's not slimy at all."

"Now do you feel a little differently about snakes?"

"Well, I'm not that afraid of them anymore," Jason said. "I guess they're even kinda cool!"

"That's great," Steve said. "I'm proud of you. Now let's see who else wants to hold the snake." This time, some of the kids volunteered.

After a long afternoon working in the field, the group returned to the log cabin. "Can I help you take care of the rest of the animals?" Jason asked.

"Sure!" Steve answered. He never tired of witnessing it—the moment of epiphany, when misunderstanding and fear of an animal changes to respect and care for that same animal. And in learning to accept misunderstood animals, the students take a giant step in learning to accept each other, and themselves, too.

Humans are judged by our appearance in the same way that animals are often judged. Koalas are looked upon more favorably than Komodo dragons. Polar bears are more desirable than piranhas. Evolutionary biologist Simon Watt is a science presenter in Great Britain, working to change opinions of less-adorable species. He developed the Ugly Animal Preservation Society to raise the profile of some of nature's more "aesthetically-challenged creatures," as he calls them. Some of the animals he highlights are the taildropper slug, the naked mole rat, and the *Promachoteuthis sulcus*, or gob-faced squid, who is a lopsided, blobby marine animal with a huge, gaping mouth in the middle of its body.

The Ugly Animal Preservation Society encourages organizations that might normally feature cute and cuddly animals as mascots to consider highlighting an ugly animal. In a world that values the beautiful, it's nice to know there are still people who love and accept Earth's less-beautiful, but equally deserving, creatures.

Accepting an animal with differences is as important as accepting people with differences. Animals have feelings and suffer pain as well as joy. An animal's eyes tell me everything I need to know. When I got my first dog, Happy, I looked deep into his soft brown eyes. I expected to see fear and hurt, and maybe there was, a little. More than that, however, I saw trust and openness. I hugged him as close to my body as I could, my ear resting against his chest. I could hear his heartbeat. Where my hands clasped, I felt the rhythm through his thin frame—a gentle thump against my skin. We were connected. I fell in love with the dog in that moment there on the doorstep. As we brought him into the house, I wondered if he felt the same toward me. Had he taken one look at my short legs and freckled face and decided he loved me all the same? Was he thankful we offered him a home—could dogs feel an emotion as complex as gratitude? One thing I didn't wonder about: Acceptance. My dog accepted me as a friend, a caretaker, a guardian. I knew it from the moment I looked into his eyes.

Accept one another, then, just as Christ accepted you,
in order to bring praise to God.
ROMANS 15:7

CHAPTER 4
RESCUE

You're my hero

All my pets have rescued me in one way
or another—saving me from loneliness, healing me from hurts,
sheltering me from life's storms. But it was a stray dog who once
rescued me in a more physical way.

During summers at home from college, I worked in a small sales
office to earn money for tuition. I disliked being cooped up at my
desk when a beautiful warm Vermont day waited outside. As the
only employee in the office, instead of sitting inside alone every
lunch hour, I took my brown paper bag and hiked into the wooded
area behind the building. In hindsight, it was foolish for a young
woman to wander in a remote area alone, but at the time I was
young and naïve, and didn't give it a second thought.

One afternoon I decided to eat beside a small, secluded pond.
As I sat enjoying the peaceful view, a shaggy dog wandered out of
the woods and sat beside me. He looked at me from under white,

curly bangs. "Hi, buddy," I said. "What are you doing out here all alone?" My break couldn't get any better—I got to enjoy the tranquil atmosphere and share my lunch with a friendly dog. He looked at me with deep brown eyes. I ruffled his ears. Although he had the whole woods in which to romp, he stayed with me.

"Want a bite?" I asked, holding out a crust of sandwich.

The dog didn't move toward the morsel of food. I noticed his muscles tighten. He let out a low growl.

I looked up to the spot in the woods where he was staring. Something moved in the bushes.

The dog nudged me and pushed me to my feet. "Okay, okay," I laughed, grabbing my empty paper sack and walking back to the path. The dog hung close to my side.

Just as we reached the edge of the woods, I looked back. There was a man, crouched behind the foliage with a camera. I realized that he'd been snapping my picture. He lifted his head and looked back at me, a menacing smile spreading across his face. A chill crept down my spine. I felt that I was looking at something sinister.

I quickened my pace. The dog escorted me the rest of the way out of the woods. What would have happened if the dog hadn't come along? To this day, I thank God for my shaggy white lunch companion.

On a different occasion, on a different continent, a giant schnauzer in England displayed amazing strength and persistent loyalty in an emergency.

LIGHTNING MONTY

Monty sniffed the air and his ears perked. The giant schnauzer always enjoyed his early morning walks. His human dad, Ian Thomas, wore shorts, a sweater, and rubber boots to traipse across the muddy terrain, and carried a metal bucket of scraps to feed the chickens and donkeys.

As mayor of the town of Redruth in Cornwall, Ian had plenty of work to do, but he always took care to tend his small farm on five acres of land, just a few miles from the coast. Monty followed. Wherever Ian went on the land, whatever he did, the strong, friendly dog was always at his side.

That day a storm was approaching. The early morning air was electric. Ian quickened his step to stay ahead of the weather.

The two had wandered a fair distance when the rain came down. Thunder sounded in the distance. Then closer. A mighty bolt of lightning flashed from the sky.

Monty yelped as he reeled backward. He'd been hit. He rose, and searched for his friend. He found him, curled up in a ball on the ground, unmoving. Attracted to the metal bucket, the lightning had struck Ian hard. He'd been blown off the ground, six feet in the air, dropped back to earth, and knocked unconscious. Monty gently licked Ian's face, as if pleading, "Wake up. Wake up."

Ian stirred, opening his eyes to Monty staring in his face. He reached out feebly to comfort his dog.

Struggling to his feet, he tried to walk, but the pain seared. He collapsed in agony. Monty brushed against him, nudging and licking his face again. Monty braced himself as Ian pulled up against the dog and wrapped his arms around Monty's neck. "Help me, Monty! Help me!"

Although dazed himself, Monty rallied. Ian managed to walk, leaning heavily on Monty for support. Monty summoned all his strength, moving forward inch by inch.

"Good boy, Monty. Good boy," Ian uttered.

The exhausted dog dragged his owner toward home, step by step across the nearly 100-yard journey. When they arrived home, they stumbled in the door. Monty retreated to a corner to recuperate, burying his head in his paws. Ian collapsed on the floor.

His panicked wife, Sharen, whisked him to the Royal Cornwall Hospital's emergency department, where he was treated, and four days later released in a lot better condition than he had arrived, though he would still require several surgeries and have a lengthy recovery.

Monty came through the incident unscathed. Ian calls his dog a gentle giant with a courageous heart. Although his rubber boots had protected Ian from an even more severe electrocution, Monty's heroics truly saved his life.

What compels animals to perform these heroic acts, even putting their own lives at risk, to save us? Is it a natural predisposition, a survival instinct, or a leftover trait from living in groups where an individual's success depended upon working together? Or, is it because they consider us family and are able to sense when we're in danger? A woman in Michigan credits her cat with saving her life.

DESPERATE MEASURES

Robin curled on the couch, a heavy knit blanket pulled over her head. She'd fallen into one of her blue moods. And that day her mood was so dark that only a miracle—a small, whiskered miracle—would save her life.

The hour was late. Robin suffered from bipolar disorder. That night, the depression was so deep, she just had to shut out the world. Her prayers had become desperate pleas. *God, don't you care about me?* Even her husband hadn't been able to ease her despair, and had gone to bed alone.

She hadn't been there for long when she felt a soft thump land beside her. Their youngest cat, a black and gray tabby, had jumped onto the couch. Cinco snuggled under her chin. She reached out and rubbed the cat's back. Warm, healing purrs vibrated next to Robin's cheek.

Right from the start, Cinco had been her heart cat. He followed her around the house. He waited at her feet when she was cooking in the kitchen and nestled in her lap when she was typing on the computer. He even joined her for prayer time, snuggling against her, comforting her with his presence, reminding her that God had gifted her with a love for cats and cats to love. Even though he was normally a shy cat, he trusted her. *Cinco cares about me*, Robin thought. Knowing that often improved her outlook.

That night, however, was different. Robin couldn't pull herself out from under the dark cloud. *Nobody understands me. Nobody wants me.* Every little hurt that she felt during the day came back and nagged at her. Every fear and worry. And she got herself into a very bad place.

When the sleep wouldn't come, Robin stood and made her way to the bathroom. Maybe a shower would wash away the blackness. She leaned against the cool tile wall under the beating water, each droplet stinging her skin. Her mind filled with thoughts. Horrible thoughts. *If only something would take away the pain.* She glanced at the razor on the edge of the tub.

The first cut raised a thin line of blood. Then, she made a second cut just above the first. As terrifying as it was, she couldn't stop herself. To deal with the amount of anguish she'd felt, the next cut would need to be very, very deep. Maybe, she thought, she could end her suffering.

As she held the razor poised above her wrist, the shower curtain rustled. Cinco's head poked around the corner. He stood there, staring.

She hesitated. She looked down at her wrist, then at the sharp razor in her other hand.

Someone does care about me. Cinco cares about me, she remembered. *And God cares.*

She set down the razor.

Wrapping a towel around her arm, she got dressed and went to the bedroom. Cinco followed closely. She awakened her husband. "I need help," she whispered.

Her husband called her doctor. While they were waiting, they prayed together. Cinco jumped up on her lap and purred.

Robin firmly believes that God heals. And for her, healing came with four paws, a caring stare, and a warm purr.

A less-common household pet, a Vietnamese pot belly pig, once devised a clever strategy to save her owner's life.

PIGGY PLAYS DEAD

The 150-pound porker lived inside the home like any other pet. Lulu ate, played, and slept with the family. She even knew how to use the doggy door in the trailer, although she could barely squeeze through. And when the family went on vacation, of course, Lulu came along.

One summer, Lulu and her family were visiting a campground. Lulu had been napping, when she heard a crash in the hall. She trotted over to find her owner sprawled out on the floor, unconscious.

Lulu waddled up and nudged the woman with her nose. There was no response. Somehow, she sensed that the woman needed attention, and that she was the only one around who could help. She squeezed out the doggy door, pushed through the gate of the fenced yard, followed the campground path, and made her way to the street.

Cars whizzed by, but none of them stopped for a pig on the side of the road.

That's when Lulu decided she had to do something drastic. She trotted out to the middle of the road and flopped down on her side.

A few cars drove around her without stopping. Lulu didn't give up. Once, she went back to the trailer and checked on the woman, and then made her way back and lay down in the middle of the road again. Finally a car stopped. The driver got out and, when Lulu jumped up, followed her to the trailer, where he found the woman and called for help.

Lulu's owner had suffered a heart attack, but thankfully help arrived in time. Lulu, the unassuming potbelly pig, was a porcine hero.

We all know that dolphins are some of the earth's most intelligent animals, and their experience living in groups likely contributes to their ability to interact with humans. Filippo the dolphin was famous in Italy. He lived in the Adriatic Sea near a popular vacation spot, surfing in the waves created by boats, often leaping and tail-walking. Other times he glided along beside swimmers, even letting them pat his slippery back.

One summer day a man and his teenage son cruised along on their pleasure boat. Alarmingly, the boy, who didn't know how to swim, fell overboard. He thrashed frantically in the deep water and began to sink. Filippo raced to the boat. He dove underneath the boy and gently pushed him up out of the water. Once they surfaced, Filippo swam to the edge of the boat so the father could grab his son and pull him to safety.

Dolphins have also rescued swimmers during shark attacks. In several instances, a pod of dolphins have formed a protective ring around an injured swimmer, keeping away the shark until help arrives.

Similarly, we are sometimes called upon to save our animal friends. Once, our adopted spaniel-mix, Kelly, needed rescuing—not from the ocean, but from the lake. And not from sharks, but from . . . ducks.

That day we were at a summer cottage where we sometimes spent weekends. Kelly had stationed herself in front of the screen window, hind legs firmly planted on the floor, front paws up on the ledge. It was her job to bark and chase away the birds and chipmunks under the feeder. She dutifully alerted us to any trespassers on "her" property. When a couple of ducks waddled up to the feeder, Kelly couldn't contain herself. She got a chance and shot out the open screen door, chasing after the surprised mallards.

Nothing could deter her from the thrill of a good chase. My husband, son, and I ran after her. She scooted down the bank, at which point the ducks took flight and landed safely out in the water. Kelly plunged in after them. Kelly can swim, but she's no athlete and has little stamina. She'd never gone deeper than a few feet from shore. Out past the lily pads, Kelly slowed. She looked at me, and I knew she was in trouble. She couldn't make it back.

Panicked, I raced to the dock and untied the rowboat. My husband and son jumped in and rowed out to rescue her. They dragged her soggy, exhausted body into the boat and rowed her back to shore. I pulled her onto the dock, and she gave herself a good shake.

"You gave me a scare," I said, hugging her soaked body.

I'm not sure, but I may have the only spaniel who had to be rescued in a rowboat.

A California rescuer had a much larger job on his hands when he learned of two whales in distress. And when the rescue looked impossible, help came in an amazing way.

# LIFTED UP

The sixteen-foot Zodiac rescue boat pounded over the waves, racing to two distressed whales about a half mile offshore from California's Palos Verdes. Peter Wallerstein and two other men had received a call about the California gray whale and her calf, entangled in a net. Peter anxiously jumped into gear. This would be his first rescue.

When they arrived, the mother and baby were wrapped so tight, they were drowning. The lightweight boat felt small and vulnerable next to the massive forty-foot whale. Peter's mind raced with everything he knew about the California gray whale. One fact stood out—they had a reputation for fighting back and overturning boats. If this whale didn't perceive their actions as friendly, they could be in big trouble. One swat of her massive tail and they'd all be crushed.

They pulled the boat up as close as they could. He leaned over the edge and used a knife to cut the net away from the mother whale. Peter marveled that she barely struggled as they worked. He hoped that she understood that they were there to help. After about fifteen minutes they got her free. The baby, however, was a bigger problem. The net was wrapped tightly around its tail. Every time it came up for air, the net dragged it down.

When you think *baby*, you think small. This baby was as big as the boat.

Peter struggled to cut the net. Just as he gripped the tangled ropes, the whale descended under the water. After agonizingly long moments, it struggled up. Peter leaned as far as he dared, but he couldn't reach. The baby started to sink again. "Don't let us be this close and not be able to save this whale," he thought.

The whale calf sank. Peter and the crew gasped as the mother whale maneuvered around the boat. Did she think they were trying to harm her baby? They clung to the edge of the boat as she dove close by. "Look!" Peter called. The calf was rising out of the water. This time, it was near enough so they could reach.

That's when he noticed that the mother whale had swum underneath the baby. She was pushing, lifting the baby up so that they could cut the ropes around her tail. Amazed, Peter and the others worked as fast as they could. The mother lifted the baby five more times, until all of the net was removed.

The message between the two had somehow been communicated. The men were there to help. The whale had assisted the men. Peter watched as the boat turned around, and the mother and baby whale swam off deeper into the ocean, safe.

Rescue personnel and good Samaritans are often seen freeing cats and dogs from ditches, rushing water, hot cars, trees, and many other dangerous situations. Once there were some trapped kittens who found themselves rescued twice in one day.

DOUBLE TROUBLE

"Where are they?" the firefighter asked.

"In the wall," came the answer.

The wall? He stepped closer and listened. Sure enough—scratching and mewing. Muffled cries. Kittens! How could they have become trapped behind the wall of a house? And, more importantly—how was he going to get them out?

The firefighter had been on dangerous calls in warehouse-sized buildings and on risky rescues where he needed all his strength and bravery to save lives. This comparatively small job with the tiny lives trapped in the wall was just as important to him. He'd give nothing less than his best. Guided by a heat-imaging camera, he and his partner cut two large holes in the wall, careful to keep a safe distance from the distressed kittens. When he reached his gloved hand through, the frightened feline squirmed farther away. "They're tucked up in there good," he told his partner. "They don't want to come out."

The kittens huddled as still as possible, as if staying trapped seemed a better option than the unknown. The firefighters tried again. Together, they managed to corral the kittens and gently lift them out of the holes. They cradled the tiny balls of fur.

When the firefighters took the kittens to the animal shelter, however, they were met with bad news. "We can take them," the shelter worker sighed, "but they'll probably have to be euthanized. I'm sorry, they're just too young."

The firefighter clutched one of the little kittens, warm in his arms. Its tiny heart beat against his chest. He couldn't let it happen. He couldn't rescue the kittens, only to have them put down! He didn't even need to think about his next move. "We'll keep 'em!" he said, turning to go out the door. "We'll take care of them at the station."

His partner nodded.

After their impulsive decision, the two men climbed into the fire truck, wondering how they'd care for their new charges. They stroked the kittens' soft fur and smiled at their tiny mews. It wouldn't be easy, with all of their other duties. The kittens, however, depended on them. They'd find a way. They drove back to the station, stopping at a pet store along the way to buy some food.

"Look!" his partner said, as they walked through the door. A cat rescue organization was set up with a table and papers, and several cats in wire cages were resting on soft towels. They walked over and explained the situation. The ladies tending the table couldn't get enough of the tiny kittens the firemen held. "They look to be only two weeks old," one of the women said. "They're going to need a lot of special care."

Deciding that the group was better equipped for the job, the firemen accepted their offer to foster the babies and, when they were old enough, find them good homes.

Some jobs are large-scale while others are smaller, but it's always just right when they have a positive outcome. And for the kittens, first saved from entrapment, and then from euthanasia, it was a purr-fect resolution.

Animals are not only rescued from imminent physical danger, but from pain, suffering, starvation, and even euthanasia as a result of abandonment. Back when I was young, there was no special term for a second-hand dog. Everyone I knew *owned* a dog. No one had *adopted* one. Today, the term *rescue dog* refers to any dog who is placed in a new home after being saved or relinquished. Even though I didn't know it at the time, I'd been rescuing dogs (and cats, rabbits, hamsters...) all my life.

Wonderful organizations and rescue groups are dedicated to saving homeless animals from the streets, neglectful and abusive situations, and high-kill shelters, and fostering them in loving homes until they are able to find their forever homes. While the job of fostering is challenging, a woman in upstate New York found that it wasn't without great rewards.

RESCUING LAKE

The new dog followed Heather Rose down the stairs to the laundry room. Heather laughed. Her own dog, Pablo, never wanted to follow her around. He was a strictly do-it-my-way dog. Her new foster dog, Lake, wanted to be with her every minute.

Heather fostered Lake for the Peppertree Rescue group in Albany, New York. Lake had come to live with her after a traumatic past. The shepherd-pit bull-boxer mix was found standing in the middle of the road, in shock. She was identified as belonging to a substandard backyard breeder. She was covered in gashes. The vet said she'd been hit by a car. And she was infested with fleas, was heartworm positive, and had serious damage to her kidneys. And, she was pregnant.

Unfortunately, the puppies didn't survive. But Lake rallied with an engaging spirit, happy wagging tail, and one ear perpetually up, the other flopped over. When Heather had met her at the transport from Georgia, Lake was the first dog off the van. She ran up to Heather and gave her a kiss, and then ran over to a bowl of food set on the curb. Since the other dogs on the van hung back, afraid, she ate all their food, too.

Now it was Heather's job to take care of Lake until she could find her a forever home.

Finding a home for Lake might not have been easy, because of her health problems. But taking into account her disposition, it would be a breeze. She got along with everyone. She wanted to play with Pablo, dancing around him, crawling close to him on his bed. Pablo just heaved a sigh, as if thinking, "You can sit there, but I'm not going to play with you." The only creature Lake didn't like was the cat—Lake was terrified of her.

Heather is a social worker. When she comes home at night, it takes a while to shake off the emotions of her job. One day she sat in the living room, weighed down by the stress of demanding consultations. She closed her eyes and took a deep breath. She felt a paw on the couch cushion beside her. Then another. Then a whole dog. Lake had climbed up beside her. She put her head in Heather's lap, as if she knew her comfort was needed. As she pet the dog, Heather felt herself relax. Despite all that Lake had been through, despite the mistreatment and neglect, and being hit by a car, and transported to a new home, the friendly little dog just wanted to give love and be loved.

Clearly, a dog rescue is always a mutually beneficial act.

One New York City woman was inspired to start her own rescue, after coming across an abandoned dog in the park.

THE DOG IN GOD'S PLANS

Sharon Azar was walking home after being interviewed to adopt a dog named Hero. Hero had been shot while protecting his human companion. All she could think about was adopting this beautiful, sweet, heroic dog who had risked his life defending the man he loved. On a whim, she took a detour through Washington Square Park.

She was passing through a quiet part of the park when she saw a dog tied to an old tree. The length of rope was so short, there was barely enough room for the big dog to turn around. He was huge, older, with thick black matted fur. The dog looked so sad, his big brown eyes pleading with her. Around his neck hung a lopsided sign, torn from a larger piece of cardboard. She winced as she read the crude black letters: "Owner died, please take dog."

Sharon never got to adopt Hero. There were many other suitors for him. But the one dog who did need her was the dog in the park, abandoned and tied to a tree. She took Baby Bear home that day, and gave him a happy, loving home. He was the dog God meant her to adopt, all along.

Hope for Paws is an animal rescue organization based in California that performs near-miracles in rescuing abandoned dogs. The founder, Eldad Hagar, creates and shares videos of his rescues. They show a man so in tune to animals that he instantly earns their trust. Fiona was one of Hope for Paws' amazing success stories. The abandoned dog had been surviving in a pile of trash in a parking lot along a strip mall in East Los Angeles. Curled up by a cement wall, the filthy, starving dog was blind, and almost lifeless, as if discarded for trash herself. Eldad and his wife rescued her, bathed her, treated her wounds, and showered her with love. A veterinarian was even able to restore the sight in one eye. For the first time in a long time, Fiona could see the trees and the grass, and the loving faces of people who cared, including the loving family who soon adopted her.

PRAYER OF A STRAY[4]

Dear God, please send me somebody who'll care!
I'm tired of running, I'm sick with despair.
My body is aching, it's so racked with pain,
And, Dear God, I pray as I run in the rain
That someone will love me and give me a home,
A warm cozy bed and a big juicy bone.
My last owner tied me all day in the yard,
Sometimes with no water and, God, that was hard!
So I chewed my leash, God, and I ran away
To rummage in garbage; and live as a stray.
But now, God, I'm tired and hungry and cold,
And I'm Oh so afraid; that I'll never grow old.
They've chased me with sticks and hit me with stones
While I run the streets just looking for bones.
I'm not really bad, God; please help if you can
For I have become just another "victim of man!"
I'm wormy, Dear God; and I'm ridden with fleas,
And all that I want is an owner to please.
If you find one for me, God, I'll try to be good;
I won't chew their shoes, and I'll do as I should.
I'll love them, protect them, and try to obey
When they tell me to sit, to lie down, or to stay!
I don't think I'll make it too long on my own,
'Cause I'm getting so weak and I'm so all alone.

Each night as I sleep in the bushes I cry,
'Cause I'm so afraid, God, that I'm going to die.
I've got so much love and devotion to give
That I should be given a new chance to live.
So, Dear God, please, Oh please, answer my prayer
And send me to somebody who will really care.

—Author Unknown

How do rescuers keep going, when there are so many animals to be helped? The question reminds me of a story I once heard about a child and a starfish. A man walking on the beach passed by a little girl picking up a starfish and gently throwing it back into the water. The tide was going out, and the starfish would die if left in the sun. She turned, and lifted another starfish. The sand was scattered with hundreds of them. The man gently asked, "Why are you bringing those starfish into the ocean? There are miles of beach, and there are so many. You'll never be able to make a difference." The child tenderly picked up a starfish and put it back into the waves and said, "It made a difference to that one."

God put animals here on earth in our care, all the "beasts of the earth," the "birds in the sky," and "every creature that moves along the ground," and "all the fish in the sea"(Genesis 9:2). We have a responsibility to care for them. We can't stand by and let them suffer or struggle in times of danger. We love them—it's all part of our amazing bond.

One of the most special dogs to share my life was our old golden retriever, Brooks. He was eleven years old when we adopted him. He'd been abandoned and left on his own for years before we came together. It was no act of heroism, no great feat of rescue that brought him into our lives; just a willingness to open our home and our hearts. His time with us was short. He died of cancer less than a year later. But the impact he made on our lives will last forever. Surely, that rescue went both ways.

Those who love me, I will deliver:
I will protect those who know my name.
Psalm 91:14 nrsv

CHAPTER 5
HEALING

Tender loving care

Growing up, I was slim; however, like many women, I battled with "baby weight," even after my kids were grown and on their own. I'd lose a few pounds, then put back on five. I'd gain a few more. Then I discovered that my dog was overweight, too.

One day I took Kelly for her checkup at the veterinarian's office. The numbers on the scale bounced up and down as she wiggled: 36, 34, 38. My eyes grew wide when the screen finally read 41.

"She's up three pounds since her last visit," the vet said, turning to me and my husband, Mike. "For a small dog like her, that isn't good. It's like fifteen pounds on a person."

"I'm feeding her less," I said.

"Are you measuring it?" the vet asked. She held up a small plastic cup and pointed to a line on it. "She should only get half a cup twice a day." Our scoop at home *definitely* held more than that. "And no table scraps," the vet continued.

Mike shot me a look. Just last night I'd given Kelly pizza crusts during dinner. "She shouldn't beg," Mike had scolded. I knew I shouldn't feed her from the table, but one look at her big brown pleading eyes and I'd given in. *A little bit won't hurt her,* I'd told myself.

The vet ran her stethoscope over Kelly's chest and abdomen. "If she doesn't lose weight, she'll be at risk for joint, skin, and heart problems, even diabetes and cancer."

Wait. Hadn't I heard that before? Just a few weeks earlier my doctor had given me the same warnings. I weighed 171 pounds— *way* too much for my five-foot frame. Gyms, health books, diets—I'd tried them all. Nothing worked.

Besides, I'd settled into a comfy routine. I worked from home, so during the day it was just Kelly and me. Only eight steps separated my office from the kitchen. How could I resist taking a break?

I'd grab cookies for me and a treat for Kelly—she deserved it for keeping me company. And exercise? I sat at the computer while Kelly followed a patch of sunlight across the floor.

I looked at my chubby dog and the vet's concerned expression. It hit me: my bad habits were hurting Kelly.

It was the beginning of a new year—the perfect time for a change, for me and my dog. First, I tackled our eating habits. At lunchtime the next day I carefully measured a half cup of Kelly's food. It hardly filled the bottom of her bowl! *I've really been overfeeding her,* I thought guiltily. I looked from her bowl to my plate where I'd made a sandwich that was almost toppling over because it was so laden with meat and cheese. *I've been overfeeding myself, too.* I remade it with an ounce of turkey, a slice of low-fat cheese, and a smear of mustard. I was surprised at how good it was.

By spring I'd learned to cook healthier. One night I was craving takeout. Instead, I made a salad with tomatoes from Mike's garden and skinless chicken breasts with green beans. "Delicious," Mike said.

I had to agree. But Kelly whined at my feet. "Can't I just give her a little treat?" I asked Mike. He shot me that look again, so I tossed Kelly a carrot. Not yet convinced, she hid it under the coffee table.

Kelly and I lost weight just by eating better. Now that the weather was nice, adding exercise was next. One May afternoon I finished work early. I looked at Kelly. She was sprawled on the back of the couch. "Time for a walk, girl," I called. Kelly barely raised her head. I tried again. "Let's go, Kel!" Kelly plodded toward me, stopping to stretch. I snapped on her leash. As soon as I opened the door, the fresh air hit us. I took a deep breath. How invigorating! Kelly's nose lifted, too. She swung her head and broke into a trot.

We walked farther than I thought we would—or could. "We'll get out every day," I promised. And we did, if it was sunny.

Then the rainy days piled up that fall. We returned to our sedentary ways, and the pounds stopped coming off. One day I glanced up from the computer and saw Kelly flopped on the couch, her big eyes sad.

Lord, Kelly trusts me and I've let her down. Myself, too. Help me. Show me how to do the right thing for us.

A few days later, I saw an ad for a used elliptical machine. I wasn't looking for one, but there it was as if it were looking for me. "What do you think?" I asked Mike.

"Great idea!" he said. "Put it in the living room." Perfect. On dismal days I'd hop on the elliptical and toss Kelly her ball. She'd run after it full tilt. Before long we were both full of energy. But it wasn't always easy.

Once I pulled an all-nighter to meet a deadline. Tired and hungry, I went into the kitchen and opened the fridge. A friend had given Mike a chocolate cake; it sat there, frosting gleaming. *I've exercised all week*, I thought. *I deserve this.*

But Kelly looked up at me with those big eyes. *Okay, Lord, I get it.* I grabbed a yogurt and gave Kelly a baby carrot. She flipped it in the air with her mouth and ate it.

Turns out Kelly and I make a great team. In just a year I lost 41 pounds and Kelly's at her goal weight, down six pounds.

These days we have a new routine: I'll work for a few hours and then march those eight steps into the kitchen. Only now I grab us both a nutritious snack. Kelly deserves a mom who will keep her healthy and stay healthy herself.

Studies show that more than 50 percent of Americans are overweight or obese. Fried and fat-laden foods and supersized portions contribute to our junk food diet, while electronic distractions keep us glued to our seats. Having a pet, however, can contribute to reducing our weight. People who share their homes with dogs tend to be more physically active and less overweight than people who don't. According to one survey, 66 percent of people with dogs exercise 30 minutes a day for at least 5 days a week.

In addition, pet parents are generally healthier than people without pets. Dog owners tend to have a lower likelihood of visiting the doctor or being on medication for sleeplessness, anxiety, and heart disease, and National Institute of Health studies have shown that pet parents who have suffered heart attacks have better recovery rates than people who don't own pets.

Here are some of the ways pets improve our health:

- **Lower Blood Pressure**
  According to studies by the National Center for Infectious Diseases, pet owners have lower blood pressure than non-pet owners. In one study of 240 married couples, pet parents had lower blood pressure and lower heart rates during rest than couples who did not have a pet. That held true whether they were at rest or undergoing stress tests. Another study showed that children with hypertension lowered their blood pressure while petting their dog.

- **Lower Cholesterol**

  Diet, exercise, and prescribed medication are often indicated to lower cholesterol. Combined with these techniques, researchers have noted lower levels of cholesterol and triglycerides in people who have pets compared to people who don't.

- **Improve Heart Health**

  One National Institute of Child Health and Human Development study involving 421 adults who had suffered heart attacks found that dog owners had a significantly better survival rate one year after having had a heart attack than those who did not own dogs, regardless of the severity of the heart attack. Owning a cat can also impact heart health. One study showed that people who never owned a cat were 40 percent more likely to die of a heart attack than those who had. Overall, pet parents have a lower risk of dying from any cardiac disease.

- **Decrease Incidents of Strokes**

  Researchers aren't sure why, but studies show that cat owners have fewer strokes than people who don't own cats. Maybe it's partly because cats have a calming effect on people. Nurturing a cat can take the owner's mind off life's stresses and worries, which can improve overall health.

- **Decrease Allergies in Children**

  This may surprise you: though many people have allergies to pet dander, studies show that children who grow up with pets actually are less likely to develop allergies than those who don't. According to a study by the University of Michigan, Henry Ford Health System, and Georgia Regents University, and funded by the National Institute of Allergy and Infectious Diseases, as long as the dog is exposed to the outdoors, the simple presence of a dog in the home can protect children from developing allergies. A child's immune system gets stronger due to higher levels of certain immune system chemicals—and this will help keep children healthier as they grow older.

- **Prevent Asthma**
  Pet allergies are one of the most common triggers of asthma, but having pets in the home can actually help prevent asthma. Studies show that children who grow up with cats are significantly less likely to develop asthma as they get older. The exception is for children whose mothers are allergic to cats—they are three times more likely to develop asthma after early exposure to cats.

- **Ease Chronic Pain**
  One breed of dog can actually ease chronic pain: the Xoloitzcuintli, or Xolo, a Mexican hairless dog. The Xolo generates such intense body heat that placing the dog against sore legs, arms, or necks can work in the same way as a heating pad or hot water bottle. The Paws for Comfort organization trains Xolos to be service dogs for people with fibromyalgia and other forms of chronic pain that respond to heat.

PATTY PAT THE MINIATURE HORSE

Most kids get the sniffles, a cough, or a sore throat now and then. But Tory gets sick a lot. A common cold could send her to the hospital, or worse, lead to serious complications. Tory has Common Variable Immunodeficiency (CVID). When Tory was five, she had bronchitis ten times in as many months. Tory's parents looked out for her, including making sure she lived a full, active life. One day, Tory's dad, Tom Russo, treated her to a visit to a friend's farm to see the miniature horses. Tory loved the miniature horses and knew most of them by name, including a rebellious young horse, Patty, who was her favorite. Tory was the first one out when the car stopped, and she ran toward the pasture.

"Watch out for Patty. She's a ramrod today," the owner cautioned. He'd had his hands full with the young, silver chestnut mare from the day he got her. "I can't do anything with that horse," he'd complain. "She never listens to me, raises Cain on the farm, and runs around like a demon."

Tory squeezed through the gate with only one thing on her mind. "Patty!" she called, clapping loudly.

Tory's mother caught up with her and grasped her small hand. "Let's go see the other horses."

But Tory shook her head firmly. "Patty Pat!" she called.

In the distance, Patty raised her head from the grass. When Tory called again, the horse perked up its ears and turned toward Tory and her mother. Then she bolted their way like a streak of lightning. No one had time to stop her. Tory's mother threw her arms around Tory as the horse bore down on them. Tom charged toward them, and the owner ran to catch the horse.

When Patty was only a breath away, something amazing happened. Instead of ramming into them or bucking, or displaying any other wild behavior, Patty stopped dead in her tracks. She whinnied softly, as if saying "hello." Her deep brown eyes stared directly at Tory. Tom watched, amazed. Something in her expression told him that she sensed she should be gentle with this child. Tory reached up and touched Patty's silky neck.

The rancher's mouth hung open. "That horse never does that for me," he said. "When I call her name, she runs the other way like a rocket!"

Patty lowered her nose and sniffed. Tory giggled. Her mother loosened her grip so Tory could reach up and hug the horse. Patty stood still and let Tory walk all around her, kissing her. Tom got choked up, seeing how tender the horse became with his daughter. The two wandered around the field together, the miniature horse and the little girl, fast friends, until it was time to go. Then Patty followed Tory to the gate.

"I don't get it," the horse's owner shook his head. "She's never done that before. For anyone. You've seen her, wild as the day she was born."

As their car pulled away, Tory twisted around in her seat, trying to see Patty. Patty pawed at the pasture gate, as if she wanted to follow them home.

From that day on, Tom brought Tory to visit Patty as often as he could. The owner even let them buy Patty and keep her at his place. Patty was just as wild as ever, except when Tory was around, and then she turned calm and docile. No one could explain it.

Tory's effect on Patty was clear. But just as amazing was Patty's effect on Tory. When Tory started school, she missed so many days due to illness, she eventually had to be homeschooled. She couldn't play contact sports or join in other active games with other kids her age. Going outside her home was awkward—sometimes she had to wear a mask to protect her from germs. Tom and his wife worried about her missing out on social life, which is so important to young girls.

When Tory saw Patty, however, everything was different. They'd pull up the drive to the farm and she'd jump out of the car, head toward the pasture and call, "Where's my Patty Pat?" Every time, the horse came galloping to her.

When Tory felt well, they ran together in the field. When she didn't feel well, Tory sat on the ground and Patty stood over her like a sentry. One time when Tory was too weak to play outside, Tom pulled up a chair so she could sit in front of the stall, and Patty pushed her nose over the door. He left them alone for a while. When he returned, Tory's schoolbooks lay open on her lap and she was reading aloud to Patty. "Dad, Patty's going to be the smartest horse in the world," Tory told him, beaming.

One day Patty suffered a devastating injury. She cut the tendon sheath on the back of her leg. She thrashed in her stall, allowing no one to change her bandages.

The horse had been thrashing and kicking, her nostrils flaring and eyes bulging. But when Tory's parents brought her to the stable, Patty's eyes softened. With her gaze glued to Tory, she let Tom help change her bandages, standing still as Tory talked and sang to her.

Tory still struggles with her illness, but whenever she gets down, she thinks about Patty and smiles. Illness after illness, treatment after treatment, she gets through and the first thing she wants to do is see Patty. It's even easier now, because Patty came to live at Tory's home! Tory can watch her best friend right from her bedroom window.

There's no way to know why Patty is calm only for Tory. Or how Tory draws strength from the little horse. But Tom knows that Patty is in his daughter's life for a reason. For hope and healing come in all forms, even in the shape of a rebellious little horse.

Then there was the teen with epilepsy who didn't want to slow down. A young service dog made sure she could stay active and independent.

INDEPENDENCE, DOODLE STYLE

Snow sprayed across Channing Seideman's cheeks as she was pulled on a sled down the ski slope. An oxygen mask covered her face. When she opened her eyes, there was Georgie, her service goldendoodle (a mix breed of golden retriever and poodle), lying atop her on the toboggan. Georgie's front feet sprawled across Channing's chest. The dog's nose pressed against the mask.

Channing had been out on a trail with the ski patrol, an internship job she'd scored. They were heading toward the chairlift when the strength left her body, her limbs unable to respond. Just like when her computer froze and needed to reboot, only with Channing it was her brain. She fell into a patroller's arms.

Channing had been diagnosed with epilepsy when she was ten years old. Seizures kept her so incapacitated that she had to miss half of middle school. Sometimes she spaced out and seemed not to be paying attention. "Are you okay?" "Are you all right?" friends and teachers asked. All the questions made her feel weird and different.

In middle school she went from earning straight A's to straight F's. As she entered high school, she'd already suffered more than forty seizures severe enough to cause her to go unconscious, turn blue, foam at the mouth, and have convulsions. She had daily twitches, jerks, headaches, and dizziness that sometimes made her walking unsteady. Her parents worried, knowing that anytime, anywhere, she could have a seizure. Every teen wants independence, and Channing was no different.

Then, when she was 17, she met Georgie.

From the day they met, Channing fell in love with the apricot goldendoodle with curly hair and long eyelashes. Georgie had been trained as a seizure response dog by Canine Assistants in Georgia. Channing already loved dogs, and she was excited to see how she and Georgie could work together to improve her life.

The first time she awoke from a seizure and saw Georgie's big wet nose in her face, and adoring eyes staring down at her, she broke out into a huge smile. "This is so much better than waking up to concerned faces and a stranger with a stethoscope," she told her mother. Somehow, Georgie made the unbearable bearable.

From then on, Georgie was always by her side. When Georgie wasn't with her, even for two minutes, she felt unprotected, like not wearing her seatbelt.

In Channing's junior and senior years of high school, Georgie became the most popular girl in school. With all the attention off Channing and onto her adorable dog, Channing felt more normal. At graduation, Georgie walked down the aisle with her and received her own diploma.

Channing tried to never let epilepsy limit her life. One afternoon, she was helping out at Cozy Point Ranch. She tied Georgie's leash to the fence rail and ran around the other side of the barn to catch a horse. When she returned, Georgie was gone. A broken section of leash dangled from the rail.

Then she spotted Georgie down by the paddock gate, sitting anxiously in a place where she could get a better view. Georgie knew her duty, and she couldn't bear to let Channing out of her sight. When the gate swung open, Georgie ran and jumped into Channing's arms. Channing laughed under the weight of the seventy-five-pound, joyfully wriggling doodle. When they were together, she felt overwhelmingly secure.

Georgie is trained to respond *after* a seizure; however, she has alerted Channing to an oncoming seizure twice. Both times she went off and found Channing's mother and brought her back. Minutes later, Channing had a seizure.

Sometimes hope built up. In her late teens, Channing had gone a long stretch without having a severe seizure. Maybe she wouldn't have another. Then came that horrible moment at the ski slope. Channing had experienced a *tonic-clonic* seizure, a major event that most often leads to unconsciousness.

But there was Georgie to help. Although the lanky dog was lying atop her on the toboggan, Channing felt no pressure. Georgie had learned to lift off all her weight. She licked Channing's hands. *You're going to be okay*, Georgie reminded her. She'd get through whatever came her way. She was safe in Georgie's paws.

A man stood in the hospital elevator along with his wife's golden retriever, Comet. The dog had been trained to respond in special ways when the man's wife had a seizure, and could even tell when an episode was about to happen.

When a mother and her daughter boarded the elevator, Comet immediately pulled toward the girl and whined. "Excuse me," the man holding the leash said, "but my wife's service dog is alerting to your little girl."

He explained that the dog behaved in that way when sensing that a person was about to have a seizure.

"No, it can't be," the mother replied. But moments later, the girl suffered a grand mal seizure. Fortunately, she received the help she needed right away.

Comet is one of many dogs trained by Jennifer Arnold, founder of Canine Assistants, a nonprofit organization near Atlanta, Georgia, to help children and adults with physical disabilities and special needs.

According to Jennifer, who has more than twenty years of experience working with a wide variety of service dogs, predicting seizures seems to be a natural ability for some dogs.

"At this point, we don't know what they're sensing," Jennifer says. "Most likely the dog is responding to an odor change."

A dog's sense of smell is at least 100,000 times stronger than a human's. Dogs mainly interpret the world by smelling objects rather than simply looking at them. A dog, Jennifer says, can detect a single drop of vanilla in an Olympic-sized pool, fourteen days later.

Not only can dogs sense an oncoming seizure, but they can be trained to assist an individual during and after the attack. The dog may lie on the person, retrieve a cordless phone, summon help from another room, or press a medic alert button.

Nearly 90 percent of the dogs who Canine Assistants places with individuals are also able to predict or react *in advance of* a seizure. When they do, they whine, paw, pace, bark, or jump. This gives the person valuable time to prepare or get help.

Trainers and scientists work with many different breeds of dogs, but they agree that the best dogs are friendly, well-behaved, and easy to train. Jennifer opts for Labrador retrievers, golden retrievers, and goldendoodles in her work. Service dogs must be calm and dependable, she says, since seizures can involve thrashing or falling down. Service dogs must not be easily frightened.

Another woman found an assistance dog not only for herself, but she also started a foundation to match dogs with others in need of healing.

MISSION PAWSIBLE

Karen Shirk stroked the ears of Ben, the sleek black German shepherd sleeping at her feet. After years of being refused, she finally had her service dog.

As a young college student, Karen had been diagnosed with Myasthenia Gravis (MG), a rare and debilitating neuromuscular disease. She endured long hospital stays and had to use a ventilator to breathe.

The only thing that kept her going was the thought of a service dog to help her gain some independence. But she was repeatedly told that dogs could not be paired with someone on a ventilator.

After failing to find an agency that could help her, Karen took matters into her own hands. She bought Ben and enrolled in training classes. Ben learned to perform many of the tasks previously performed by personal care assistants, such as picking up objects and opening doors.

Sharing her life with Ben made her ask, "How many others are turned away because they don't fit the service dog agencies' criteria? How many others need the same miracles that Ben offers me?"

That's when she decided she would do something to improve the quality of life for others with severe handicaps by providing them with service dogs.

Based on her and Ben's success, Karen started her own agency, 4 Paws for Ability, in 1998, which provides service dogs to any child with a disability who wishes to have a dog.

Most agencies turn down children, feeling that children can't handle service dogs alone. "Which is true. They can't," Karen says. "But we work with kids by having the parents handle the dog, at the same time getting the dog bonded to the child, not the handler."

4 Paws for Ability trains dogs to help children with autism, Down syndrome, diabetes, seizures, cancer, hearing impairment, loss of mobility, mental health impairments, and many other conditions.

One of Karen's most rewarding experiences was with a five-year-old boy named Connor. He had severe medical issues and was on a ventilator, as she had been. Through the love and assistance of his service dog, Casey, he grew stronger, gained independence, and could finally go outside and play.

4 Paws for Ability raises and trains their own dogs, generally working with breeds such as golden retrievers, collies, German shepherds, labradoodles, and papillons. In 2000, Karen expanded her enterprise by establishing Mission Pawsible, a program to teach prison inmates to help socialize and train puppies.

"It's so cool to see how much difference the dogs make for the inmates," she says. "Even though these men and women are locked away from society, they can do something good."

Karen recalls a middle-aged inmate who had been involved in a murder when he was eighteen. He told her that the dog helped ease his stress and build his confidence and self-esteem.

When troubles are at their peak, God can do wonderful things. Karen found a way to help not only herself, but also hundreds of others—all thanks to a nudge from a devoted German shepherd and the countless other service dogs who make her mission *pawsible.*

Some dogs are trained to sniff out cancer. The pooches' results may be more accurate than some medical tests currently being used. Comparing the dogs' results with current diagnostic methods could lead to improved cancer detection.

Michael McCulloch, director of research at the Pine Street Foundation in California, is conducting groundbreaking research on this subject. In one study, he collected breath samples from individuals with lung and breast cancer, along with samples from those without. To train the dogs, he presented them with a target sample (one with cancer cells) and once they sniffed, they were offered a reward of food, affection, or play.

The dogs then sniffed several samples—some with cancer, some without. When they smelled lung or breast cancer, they responded by sitting beside the appropriate sample. The dogs were right 99 percent of the time.

Michael works with many breeds, including miniature poodles, standard poodles, Labrador retrievers, and Portuguese water dogs. "Any breed of dog has the genetic makeup to be a good sniffer," he says. "Temperament and work ethic of the dog makes the biggest difference."[5]

Dogs helping people is nothing new, but using dogs to sniff out cancer and predict seizures is on the cusp of medical breakthrough. Why is this significant? According to Michael, "The most important point is that this establishes that exhaled breath could be a valid diagnostic tool." Researchers, says Michael, now have to figure out how to analyze breath samples for cancer and aim for the success rate of the dogs.[6]

While animals help keep us well, we often return the favor to the animals we love. Rehabilitators save wildlife, farmers care for their stock, and veterinarians treat ill and injured animals. As pet parents, it's our responsibility to tend to the health of our pets.

Betsy Banks Saul is not only the founder of Petfinder, the most successful animal rescue site in the world, but she also enjoys spending time on her farm in North Carolina, where she discovered that a chicken just needed a little help to feel better.

CLUCK, CLUCK, WHEEZE

Tia huddled under a bush, gasping for breath. Betsy knelt, scooped the chicken into her hands, and rushed the distressed bird to the veterinarian's.

The little chicken wasn't the friendliest creature she'd ever met. Tia was often irritable and standoffish. She didn't like to be handled. Betsy had found the chicken, along with two others, weak and starving, abandoned in the park. How they got there, she had no idea. They'd had their beaks trimmed—a cruel practice frequently used in factory farming. Her heart ached to see the innocent creatures cast aside, unwanted. Now they were pets. The two other chickens loved following Betsy around and playfully pecking at her shoes. But not Tia.

The veterinarian examined the chicken, and after a CAT scan and other tests revealed nothing, guessed that the bird had allergies or something wrong with her heart. Betsy had adopted an asthmatic chicken.

If someone had already discarded the chickens, thinking they were of no value, what might someone do with a chicken with allergies? Betsy knew the answer. She, however, had different plans. She carried the chicken into her house and rigged up a new home—an extra-large dog crate. She administered antihistamines, antibiotics, and other medication. She didn't expect the chicken to make it. These measures would, at least, keep her comfortable.

Tia's allergies didn't clear up right away. She sneezed so hard, she knocked herself off her feet. If Betsy put grain in her cage that hadn't been rinsed, the dust would make Tia gasp for air.

"She needs more oxygen," Betsy sighed. She ordered a used oxygen machine online and anxiously waited for it to arrive.

The next day Betsy lugged a heavy oxygen machine into the house. She held Tia and placed the tube next to her stubby beak. As Tia inhaled the oxygen, her body relaxed and she stopped gasping. It worked! Her comb and waddle almost immediately turned bright red, like her healthy sisters' did!

She put Tia back in the crate, dragged the tank alongside the enclosure, and pulled the tube through the wires. Maybe, somehow, it would help. The very next day, she noticed something amazing. When Tia seemed to sense an attack coming on, she skittered over and stood by the machine, softly pecking and sucking the end of the tube. Before long, it wasn't unusual to find Tia standing there, beak to the tube. Betsy didn't have to listen for Tia's gasps to bring her oxygen—the chicken would treat herself!

On Tia's good days, she walked around the office, sat atop Betsy's desk, and "helped" with the paperwork. Although it wasn't comfortable for Tia to be outside for extended periods of time, Betsy brought her to the yard for an hour each day, where Tia enjoyed scratching and pecking with the other chickens. When she felt her allergies get the best of her, she strutted over, climbed into Betsy's lap, and laid her head on her knee.

Just like people, not every animal is always fun, loving, and sociable. Betsy had thought Tia was a cranky, aloof chicken, but all along she was actually feeling ill. Once Betsy understood Tia's medical condition and provided appropriate care, Tia became the best and friendliest little chicken companion anyone could want.

Our pets depend upon us to make sound decisions about their health. Managing her cat's disease led one woman to understand her father's illness as well.

ONE DIAGNOSIS, TWO TREATMENTS

The cat squirmed. Oh, how she hated needles! Melissa Robinson held the syringe, biting her lip. She had even been a little dizzy at the doctor's office. The thought of poking a needle into her sweet cat Tara sent shivers down her spine. Although the vet tech had trained her how to administer the shot with a drop of harmless water, now she was alone. How could she do this?

Days earlier, when she'd brought Tara to the veterinarian's office, she had no idea things would end up so grim. The cat had been drinking excessively and peeing like crazy, too. Antibiotics hadn't cleared things up. Then there was blood. The vet tech ran some tests. While Melissa waited for the results, she spoke softly to Tara. "Everything's going to be alright."

But then, everything wasn't okay. The blood sugar levels came back sky high. Tara had diabetes.

"Do you think you can give her insulin shots?" the tech had asked.

Melissa wanted to shout, "No!" No way could she do this. Then she looked at her cat, ears back, scared. Sick. If Tara needed shots, that's what she would get.

That morning, however, standing there, with the moment before her, Melissa wasn't so sure. What if she did it wrong? What if she hurt Tara? Her father walked into the kitchen and put his weathered hand on her shoulder. It felt warm, encouraging. Her father had grown up on a dairy farm. He'd given shots to cows hundreds of times. She admired her father. If he could do it, so could she. Carefully, she guided the needle into the scruff of Tara's neck. Tara accepted her treatment calmly. She didn't even flinch.

"Good girl," Melissa said.

Each day, administering the shot became easier and less stressful. Tara was a forgiving patient. The medication improved Tara's energy level and her thirst decreased. Melissa even learned how to test Tara's blood sugar levels by pricking her ear and to graph her results to determine effectiveness and manage dosing.

After every treatment, Melissa hugged her cat close and told her she loved her. "This cat needs me so much," Melissa thought. "I'll never let her down." Tara purred.

A few months later, Melissa's father returned from a doctor appointment. He sat down in the kitchen and picked up the cat, stroking her back. "I guess I'm just like you," he said. "I just found out I've got diabetes, too."

"Oh no, Dad. What did the doctor say?"

It turned out that for the time being, he only had to monitor his glucose with finger sticks. Melissa reached for Tara's meter and showed her father how to test his sugar levels. By researching Tara's diabetes, she'd learned a lot that could help her father as well. She would do everything she could to make sure he was okay. And, if it ended up that he should need help administering insulin injections some day, could she do it?

She only had to take one look at Tara to know the answer.

A Banfield Hospital study reports that 16 percent of cats and 32 percent of dogs are diagnosed with diabetes. With symptoms such as excessive thirst, excessive urination, increased appetite, and weight loss, a diagnosis of diabetes can be worrisome. Fortunately, diabetes is highly manageable with the proper care and medication, and most pets live a full, long life.

Cancer is the leading disease-related cause of death in pets, but experts say that more than half of all cancers are curable if caught early. Sometimes the disease appears suddenly, and treatment takes dramatic forms, as with Jackie Bouchard's mixed breed dog Abby.

TRI-PAWED

It's just a limp, Jackie reminded herself. Abby, her lean and long-legged shepherd-collie mix, was young and full of energy. Nothing to worry about.

Then the phone rang, and the vet delivered the test results. "Osteosarcoma," she said.

Bone cancer.

Jackie hung up the phone and crouched beside her dog. How could this be? Abby was just over a year old. She seemed fine, except for the limp that had developed a few weeks earlier and a small lump that seemed to have shown up overnight. How could Abby be sick? And, not just sick, but dying.

Jackie and her husband had adopted Abby almost a year earlier. The four-month-old puppy was all fuzz and fluff. Dark markings on her face looked like dramatic Cleopatra eyeliner. Abby's zest and enthusiasm soon stole their hearts. Every day she pawed at her pink leash, begging for a car ride to her favorite place—Fiesta Island, a dog beach with 100 acres of sandy beach and calm water. Seeing her romp and play filled Jackie with contentment.

Now, would they ever be able to go to Abby's favorite place again?

The vet offered several options, none of which were clear-cut or easy. "Can we really do this?" Jackie asked her husband, after making the difficult decision. "Can Abby?"

They'd decided on amputation.

One week later, Jackie brought her dog in for surgery. To hold back the tears, she reminded herself that this would give Abby the best chance at a full life. If all went well, Abby would be strong, healthy, happy, and free of cancer.

Waiting was agonizing, but at last the vet gave her the news that the procedure had gone well. The next day they were allowed to see her. "Be prepared," the vet said. "She's going to look like Frankenstein's dog."

She sure did. A gigantic incision formed a big Y-shape on Abby's shoulder. Rows of staples held it together. Jackie swallowed hard. Abby wagged her tail as if to say, "Everything's going to be all right."

"My brave girl," Jackie said.

After only one overnight at the veterinarian's office, Abby was ready to go home. "Will we carry her out?" Jackie's husband asked.

"Oh no, she's already beyond that." The nurse showed them how to help Abby walk with a sling under her chest. Jackie's husband took hold of the leash, while Jackie handled the sling. As soon as they opened the clinic's front door, Abby bolted for the grass. Trying to keep up, Jackie stumbled, Abby's legs got tangled in the sling, and the dog face-planted on the lawn. Poor thing! Not a very good start.

A few days later, however, Jackie was having a hard time keeping Abby still. At first Jackie had tried to help with the sling, but Abby did better on her own. She learned to compensate for her lost leg and hopped around competently on three. Abby also received a course of chemotherapy treatments by IV. Fortunately, she tolerated them well, and she even came to love the attention she received at the clinic.

The recovery wasn't without challenges, lots of them. While Abby was managing physically, Jackie wondered how she was adjusting emotionally. One day she reached for her, and Abby yelped. "I'm not even touching her incision!" Jackie told her husband. Abby hobbled into the corner and sulked. Other times she'd move away, and curl up in the farthest corner of the room. "I feel like she's mad at me," Jackie sniffed. She tried not to assign human emotions to a dog, but she felt like Abby was angry that she'd allowed the doctors to amputate her leg. Had she made the right decision? Thankfully, in time Abby's aloofness went away. She bounced around the house with the same mischievous rambunctiousness she'd always had. She could do everything post-amputation that she did before.

She even loved taking her walks around the neighborhood, basking in the California sunshine. Abby always captured attention.

Once a little boy took a long look at Abby's missing leg. "Will it grow back?" he asked. Another time, a man stopped his car and rolled down the window. "I love your dog!" he called. Jackie smiled. She didn't want people feeling sorry for Abby. She wanted them to see how well dogs could do on three legs.

One friend, however, was not so kind. He sent Jackie a message: "What you're doing is cruel. You should put her down and end her misery." Jackie pushed away the hurt. Abby wasn't miserable.

This is what she wanted her friend to see: the day she took Abby back to Fiesta Island for the first time. As they neared, Abby bounced around in the back seat. "We're almost there!" she seemed to say.

Jackie parked the car and snapped on Abby's pink leash. She called it her "warrior princess" color. On the beach, she unhooked the leash, and Abby took off running, chasing the shadows of seagulls that appeared on the hot sand. Her friends were there, too—dogs she used to play with. They all recognized her, wagged their tails, and took off together, racing up and down the sandy strip.

"Does she look miserable to you?" Jackie wanted to ask her friend.

As if in answer, Abby came running up to her, full tilt, a huge grin on her face.

The Morris Animal Foundation has invested more than $70 million toward more than 2,000 animal health studies that have improved the quality of life for dogs, cats, horses, and wildlife in more than 150 countries around the world. One of the largest and longest studies ever conducted in veterinary medicine is their Golden Retriever Lifetime Study. More than half of golden retrievers develop cancer. This study's goal is to follow 3,000 golden retrievers to determine the genetic, environmental, and nutritional risk factors for cancer and other canine health problems, and learn how to better prevent, diagnose, and treat cancer and other canine diseases.

My son's golden retriever puppy, Zeke, is a new volunteer for the Morris Animal Foundation Golden Retriever Lifetime Study. I'm proud that this little guy will be a part of helping to find a cure for a disease that has claimed two golden retrievers in our family. What a special way to pay it forward.

Healing can take all forms. Susan Karas looked to her spiritual strength to help her senior dog.

HEALING OILS

The tiny white teacup Maltese trembled. Gucci wouldn't eat, not even his favorite treats with the real bone marrow in the center. He curled in his bed, sides heaving. That evening, Gucci hacked and wheezed. "I have to do something. I can't let him go on this way," Susan groaned. She scooped her pup up in a warm blanket and rushed him to the vet's office.

"I'm so sorry," the doctor said, moving the stethoscope across the dog's chest. "His heart disease isn't any better. Now there's fluid in his lungs. We can try a new medication. It might improve his breathing. Gucci's old and tired. I've done all I can do."

How could she even think of being without Gucci, the pup who was so small, she attached a silver bell to his collar so she'd know where he was and wouldn't step on him? Gucci, the gentle dog who loved to float beside her on an inflatable raft in the swimming pool? Or the playful guy who dropped his yellow ball at her feet and delighted in chasing it across the kitchen? She lifted him from the cold examining table and hugged him. "Thank you, Doctor."

Susan took him home and cared for him, each day clearing his untouched dinner bowls and administering his medication. The dog panted and rested his face on his paws. She didn't want the dog to suffer, but she wasn't ready to say goodbye. What was the right thing to do? The vet had done everything he could for Gucci. Even with the medications, he wasn't getting better. Was there any place she hadn't turned? That night she couldn't sleep, worrying about her sweet dog.

The next day was Sunday. As Susan sat in church listening to the organ music, she couldn't get her mind off her pup at home. A glimmer of light beamed through the stained glass window to a cruet on the altar. At church, they anointed the sick with oil. God healed people. Would he heal dogs, too?

After the service, she went home and right to the kitchen cupboard. There was a small bottle of olive oil. She turned and looked at the frail dog on his pillow and swallowed hard. She whispered a prayer, poured a small amount onto her fingertip, and dabbed the oil across his head. *God, please heal this little dog. Keep him in Your hands. I'm not ready to let him go. But Thy will be done.*

That night she had her first restful sleep in weeks. She'd done all she could. Whatever happened, she had no control. He was in God's hands.

Over the next few weeks, Gucci appeared no better. He slept in his bed, his breath ragged. "It's just not to be," she thought sadly. Once she even reached for the phone. Then she hung up abruptly. She couldn't bring herself to make that appointment. Not yet.

Every day Gucci seemed the same.

Then, one day Susan walked into the kitchen and there was Gucci, sitting on the tile floor. Susan gasped and then grinned. His eyes shone. The tip of his tail wagged. He was obviously feeling better that day, and whether it was for a moment or a month, or a year, it was a gift she wouldn't take lightly. God had granted them more time together.

Then she noticed—Gucci held his favorite yellow ball in his mouth. She crouched. He dropped the ball at her feet. "Let's play," she smiled.

He tipped his head to the side as if in agreement: *Let's play!*

My dogs have contributed to improving my health, not just by helping me lose weight. I have high blood pressure. My doctor monitors my numbers, but last year for a time, my medication wasn't working. I wondered if my uncontrolled high blood pressure was putting me at risk for a stroke or heart attack. The more I thought about it, the more anxious I became. Of course, it always seemed worse at night.

"I don't feel well," I told my husband one evening. I certainly didn't look like I felt well. I crossed my arms over my stomach.

Mike put his arm around my shoulder and pulled me close. "You'll be fine. You have a re-check in a few days. The doctor is on this."

His words comforted me, but not for long. That night, I lay in bed staring at the curtains fluttering as a breeze blew through the window. With each flutter, a new worry squirmed into my mind. *What if the doctor missed something? What if my numbers were more elevated than he thought? What if I was getting worse? What if...what if...what if...*

I squirmed, tossed, turned, and then sat up straight. My throat tightened, my breath came in rapid gasps. All those "what ifs" started to feel very real. My heart raced. "Mike, I don't feel right," I said. The bedroom seemed to spin.

Mike had tried to console me a thousand times before. This time, I'd really worked myself up. Now his words weren't calming me at all. I felt like I was going to pass out.

Mike patted the bed. "Come here, Ike." He called our golden retriever up onto the bed. Instinctively, the dog curled beside me, sending warmth to my body.

"Pat the dog," Mike said.

I reached out and stroked Ike's soft golden fur. I ruffled his ears. As I patted, my anxiety eased. My breathing came under control. The worried thoughts dissipated. I leaned back, ready to sleep again.

"What made you think to do that?" I asked, my eyelids drooping. "It really helped."

"You know all that research you did about dogs and health? You told me that dogs can lower blood pressure."

"It must have worked," I said, my eyes heavy. I didn't feel my heart racing anymore. I didn't need to take my blood pressure to know. A dog was good for my health.

In return, I do whatever I can to keep my pets in good physical shape, especially by providing boundless love to keep my best friends happy and healthy every day.

So they set out and went from village to village,
proclaiming the good news and healing people everywhere.
LUKE 9:6

CHAPTER 6
COMPASSION

You've got a friend in me

The dog was for our son.

That's what I thought.

Our daughter was heading off to college in the fall. The house would be different without her. Lonely. He'd miss his sister. The dog would help him.

I sat at my computer, pouring over the rescue group listings when one sweet, furry face captured my heart: a small female spaniel with big brown eyes and long ears.

"This dog is for Andy, right?" my husband asked, looking over my shoulder. "Wouldn't he prefer a Lab or a boxer? Something more, uh, manly?"

True, our teenage boy might enjoy a big dog to run around with. Then again, Andy might also like a snuggly pup. Who wouldn't? She looked as cuddly as a newborn baby, as if she were reaching out to me, begging me to hold her close. I picked up the phone and called the number of the rescue group.

We arranged to meet the dog, Kelly, with her foster mom. She was about one year old, with brown, red, and cream-colored fur flowing in all directions. She sat there like such a little lady, dainty paws crossed, long silky ears that looked as if you could tie them up with bows.

She was the one.

Kelly settled into our household easily. Andy loved having a dog of his own. Sometimes he cuddled her on the couch as he watched the sports channel. Other times he took her outside to play. She loved going outside; however, she had no intention of running, jumping, or chasing after dirty old tennis balls. When a friend would come over for a pickup game of basketball, Andy would be off.

More and more, Andy grew busy with school, sports, and activities. With our daughter in college and Andy increasingly occupied, I felt the emptiness magnify. "Everything's changed," I told my husband one night. Kate and I used to give each other manicures, talk about boys and the books we'd read, and laugh about things that happened at school. I missed that. "The kids are grown. Kate's away. Andy will be next."

"Change isn't bad. It's just different," he said, hugging me tight.

I didn't like different. I couldn't get over the emptiness. The next day as I worked in my home office, I sulked. The nest was practically empty, and where did that leave me?

As I tapped at my computer, Kelly wandered up and sat beside my chair. She nudged my leg, and I absently reached down and stroked her soft head.

She continued to do this every day, resting beside me as I worked. Sometimes I took a break and we played with her pink bunny toy. Other times we went outside. I didn't like running around playing with tennis balls either, so we would walk.

After a walk, I came inside and passed my daughter's open bedroom door. This was where we'd chatted after dinner, where we'd worked out life's little problems. Now, the room was too neat. Empty. Just like I felt inside, without Kate at home.

As I stood there lost in my thoughts, Kelly padded up and nudged my leg. I crouched down on the floor beside her and stroked her neck. With each motion, some of the heaviness escaped. Even though she was Andy's dog, Kelly sensed that *I* was the one who needed her.

I guess it was no mistake that I'd chosen a sweet little girl dog— deep down, I knew I'd be missing my daughter. All along, the dog was meant for me. With Kelly's compassionate love, I'd get through the transition as my kids grew and flew from the nest.

Compassion requires thinking beyond oneself and responding to the needs and emotions of others. Are animals capable of compassion? *National Geographic* documented a compelling case in their 2006 wildlife film *Eye of the Leopard*.

A young female leopard had made her first kill and was about to devour the baboon, when she discovered a baby clinging to its dead mother. The leopard abandoned her meal and gently carried the baby to safety up a tree, nestling it to keep it warm. Unfortunately, the baby baboon wasn't able to survive without its mother, but not for the leopard's lack of trying. Other cases include a dog in Australia who rescued a baby kangaroo from the pouch of its mother who had been hit by a car, and a hippo who saved a zebra and a wildebeest from drowning. These unusual instances seem to be acts of compassion.

A CAT NAMED BIRD

Bird was a cat, a soft shade of silver with a long, expressive tail. His human was a teenager named Caitie.

Bird came into Caitie's life when the fourteen-year-old was in her first remission from leukemia.

Caitie's parents had suggested the idea of adopting a cat, figuring the young lady needed something positive and nurturing in her life. When Caitie went to select her new friend, all the kittens were let loose into the room. Bird took one look at Caitie, walked over, and sat in her lap. Bird chose Caitie.

From the moment they were together, Bird was constantly at Caitie's side. She was his person. Bird sat with Caitie as she did her homework and read her favorite books. Caitie loved to write, and her cat was the subject of many of her stories. When Caitie was away at school, Bird sat by the window and waited for her to come home. He sat in her lap, purring as she did her homework. "I love you, Bird," she'd say.

When Caitie felt discouraged, she'd talk to Bird, telling him things she couldn't bear to share with anyone else. Sometimes, she'd pull one of her old baby dresses over Bird's head, finding comfort in childish things. Bird never complained. He tolerated the game because he loved Caitie. And he could rock a pink smocked dress with dignity. *I own this*, he seemed to say.

Caitie grew weak and tired. Her bed was moved downstairs to the living room. Bird stood guard, protecting her from an unseen enemy. At night, the cat joined her in her bed, starting out by her feet. In the morning, his head would be next to hers on the pillow.

Sometimes, Caitie seemed better and Bird would grab a toy for her to play with him. At times when she had to go to the hospital, she'd be away for days, even weeks. Bird wandered around the house, calling for her. Then Caitie's father noticed Bird do something unusual. The lonely cat would find Caitie's favorite clothes and nestle in them. He'd snatch anything that he knew she loved.

Once, when Caitie and her mother returned from the hospital, they found a pile of treasures, topped by Caitie's favorite writing pen. Bird slept right beside the pile.

Eventually, Caitie grew worse. Her parents and the doctors did everything they could, but the cancer couldn't be beat. One terrible night, EMTs were called. When the strange men arrived, Bird tried to get near Caitie, but there was too much commotion. She was being taken off in a stretcher, her parents following. Bird watched for a moment, ears tucked back, frightened. Then he scurried and hid under Caitie's bed.

That night Caitie didn't return. Her mother and father sat in the quiet living room, sobbing, bereft. In shock. Bird paused by Caitie's empty bed. He stood for a long time, taking in what his senses would allow. Overwhelming grief hung over the house. How could parents ever recover from the loss of a child?

Finally, Caitie's mother staggered to her room and tried to sleep.

Late in the evening, Bird appeared in the doorway. Bird had never spent much time in the parents' bedroom before. He'd never been on their bed or slept with them.

Bird approached and put his front feet on the side of the bed. Slowly, he climbed up next to Caitie's mother and put his face on hers, rubbing at her tears. He crawled underneath the blanket and curled up by her stomach. He stayed there, very still, comforting her all night long.

Dayna Hilton is a volunteer firefighter with the Johnson County Rural Fire District #1 in Arkansas and Executive Director of the Keep Kids Fire Safe Foundation. Traveling the country, she and her dalmatian, Molly, specialize in teaching children how to stay safe in the event of a fire. What she wasn't prepared for was how Molly also helped reach out in compassion to a shy young man.

A SPECIAL MESSAGE

He stood in the back of the crowd. Dayna hadn't noticed him at first, he was so quiet and still. The tall young man was part of a small group who approached Dayna at an event at the Bloomington, Illinois, Children's Discovery Museum. She and Molly had been handing out Molly's trading cards. The group eyed them curiously.

"Hello!" Dayna greeted, drawing them closer. "Come on over! I'm Firefighter Dayna and this is Molly the Fire Safety Dog. Do you know what to do in the event of a fire in your home?"

The young men and women smiled and nodded, but no one answered. Dayna quickly realized that they were hearing impaired. "Hi!" she signed, and the group smiled even broader. She spotted the interpreter for the group. "Would they like to pet Molly?" she asked.

When the interpreter communicated the message to the excited group, they approached Molly one by one. Each of their touches appeared deep and meaningful. Molly sat patiently. She was used to being the center of attention and loved her job. Dayna merely stood back and watched.

Then she noticed the tall boy in the back of the group. He was a little heavier than the others and awkward. He shifted his weight on his feet, as if he wanted to come closer, but wasn't confident enough to try. Dayna saw a soft flicker of light in his eyes. She motioned for him to come forward.

Hesitantly, he approached. He looked at Molly with the broadest smile Dayna had ever seen. His hand reached out. He gently touched Molly's head. Molly sat very still, leaning into his legs. She let him scratch her ears and chin. He ran his hands down her back and sides. She stared up into his face and he stared back at her. It was as if only the two of them existed. Something passed between them in that moment. A tingle went down Dayna's spine—she knew she'd just witnessed something special.

What Molly had communicated to the boy, Dayna couldn't be sure. She hoped the dog had sent the message that he was worthy and loved. She blinked back tears, emotions spilling over.

As the group walked away, the young man turned and signed, "Thank you!"

Dayna returned the sign.

Molly tilted her head, her tongue hanging out to the side, looking after the young man. She had no words to speak and the young man had no ability to hear. Yet their communication had been perfect.

There are animal anti-cruelty laws in all 50 U.S. states, with penalties that include fines or prison time. It's easy to focus on the heinous acts of individuals who abuse or neglect animals. The only way not to be overwhelmed by these sad stories is to realize that there are even more compassionate people who are devoted to carrying out acts of kindness toward animals every day, just because it's the right thing to do.

Understanding what an animal needs is key to helping that animal live a better quality of life, as Betsy Banks Saul discovered with her asthmatic chicken, Tia. Another chicken in Betsy's household found that the luckiest pets aren't only those who receive Betsy's help through her website, Petfinder.com, but also those who end up in her own backyard.

BROODY HEN

Betsy reached into the nesting box, only to be loudly scolded by a pretty young Wyandotte hen. *Leave me alone*, the hen seemed to say. *Can't you see I've got work to do?* Puffed up like a turkey, the hen had stockpiled eggs, but her efforts were futile. There was no rooster, and none of the eggs were fertilized. She just sat there, waiting for her imaginary brood to hatch.

The next day Betsy trudged down to the hen house. There the stubborn hen sat. Betsy couldn't leave her there to her useless nesting. She lifted the hen from the box, fighting off angry pecks to her arms, and carried her out to scratch in the dirt with the other chickens. Before long, however, the hen skedaddled back to the hen house and resumed her maternal duties. Betsy sighed—it hurt to see the hen devotedly sitting there.

Betsy tried everything to dissuade the wannabe-mama. She began to worry about the hen's health, too—she was so dedicated to sitting on the nest, she'd refused to eat or drink.

A few days later, Betsy noticed an abandoned clutch of Guinea fowl eggs along the fence row. Guinea fowl were notoriously bad mothers. She bent and lifted one of the small, hard, teardrop-shaped eggs. It was as if the perfect solution was placed there, right before her eyes. There were the eggs without a mama to care for them, and there was a hen who dearly wanted to be a mother. Maybe there was a way.

She gathered up the eggs, gently carried them to the hen house, and placed them in the nest. The overjoyed hen proudly went to work, at once satisfied with her duty. Betsy still worried. This was all well and good for now, but what if none of the eggs hatched? Were they even fertilized? Only time—approximately 28 days—would tell.

On day 27 Betsy walked out to the hen house. Did she hear soft peeping? Could it be? She gently lifted the hen. There was a cloud of soft, puffy baby Guinea chicks!

Mama, as Betsy named the hen, truly lived up to her name. She found the juiciest worms for her babies. She chopped her oats into tiny bits that fit in their tiny beaks. She took them for walks around the yard. Betsy watched, blinking back tears. She wanted the best for her hen, even if it hadn't been her own plan.

The chicks thrived, all because of a tenacious broody hen, and a woman who was compassionate enough to give the hen her heart's desire.

A family in Troy, New York, believed in helping critters find a nice place to live, even if it meant providing the home.

THE CAT HOUSE

Simon scratched at the door. No matter what she did, Ruth Hunter's aging orange and white tabby was not happy inside. He seemed to always want to go out, and since they had a fair amount of property, it seemed reasonable to let him roam. But Ruth worried that her beloved cat would get cold outside at night.

"Let's get him a cat house," she said. "Something nice."

"A house for a cat? He'll be okay outside, won't he?" Ken asked, although he knew it would do no good. His wife wouldn't stop worrying until they came up with a snug home for the cat to spend the nights.

They bought the sturdiest structure they could find. Ruth, however, wasn't finished yet. First, she insulated it with foam all around the outside. Then she fastened a towel over the door to keep out the drafts. She put the little house on a nice wicker chair on the front porch, where Simon could come and go as he pleased.

"Here's the finishing touch," Ruth said, running an electrical cord out the living room window, and placing an electric heating pad inside. "Now he'll be nice and warm."

"You're kidding!" Ken sighed.

Simon took to the house right away. Every night Ruth went outside to say goodnight, reaching her hand inside the door and stroking his fur. "Sleep tight," she'd say. Then she'd return to her own house, secure that the cat was comfortable, safe, and warm.

One night Ruth went out to say goodnight to Simon. Strange—Simon didn't come out to greet her like usual. She reached her hand inside the house to pat the cat. Something felt off—the cat's fur felt coarse and oily. *Maybe he'd gotten into something?* Then a strange, musky smell rose up. *Was Simon sick? Injured?* She crouched, peering through the little door.

Ruth snatched her hand away and squealed. "Oh no!"

The thing that was not Simon hissed.

Ken and one of their sons came running out with a flashlight. They shined it inside the doorway. There, curled up in the cat house, on the electric heating pad, was a fat old opossum.

That night Ruth brought Simon inside. But what would happen next? Simon wanted to be outside. She didn't want to remove the cat house and take away Simon's warm quarters. Hopefully, the opossum wouldn't return.

The next night, however, as she cautiously went out to say goodnight to Simon, there was the stinky old opossum's rump and furless tail sticking out of the cat house door. "This isn't your home," she scolded. "Get out!" She tipped the chair, hoping it would spill him out. Bravely, she lifted the box and gave it a good shake. The opossum held firm. He wasn't about to vacate the plush premises.

"Ken," she said when she returned to the house. "We're going to have to do something about that opossum."

A few days later she went outside to say goodnight to Simon. He was there, snug inside his cat house. A new cat house. This one was even better, made of a large box, insulated and covered with a quilt, with new soft blankets and a fresh heating pad. "Sleep tight," she said.

As she walked back inside, she stopped at the original cat house. She'd moved it onto the floor and had taken out the blankets and heating pad, making it not-so-cozy. But the critter (which her son had named Dale) still enjoyed the accommodations. She didn't have to stick her hand inside to know. Dale's long, pink tail hung out the door. He knew a good thing when he found one.

Everyone seemed happy with the solution. Two cat houses. Or rather, a cat house and an opossum house. After all, Dale was a creature of God's, and who was she to cast him out?

When most of us come across a slithering, poisonous, or creepy creature, our reaction is to run away. Not so for spider naturalist Sheryl Smith-Rodgers. Her faithfulness toward animals extends even to some who make others uncomfortable.

ALL GOD'S CREATURES

A dark blob lay in the road up ahead, about the size of her hand. As the car drew closer, Sheryl could see that the object was moving.

"Slow down, James," she said, leaning toward the window to get a better view.

Her husband stepped on the brake. "Sheryl! Are you sure you want to save *that*?"

The car stopped just in front of a large, hairy, black tarantula

Sheryl had loved creepy crawly things ever since she was a little girl. She remembers a little spider who'd lived in her family's mailbox. She'd never dreamed of squishing it—she used to go outside and talk to it instead. And then there was the cobweb spider named Springy, who'd lived in the corner of the shower. When she was four, her Sunday school teacher even gave her crawly animals. She took them home in a glass jar with some grass and cared for them like any beloved pet.

Most of her friends didn't understand Sheryl's affinity for arachnids. She'd patiently explain a spider's role in the ecosystem, keeping insects in balance. Once, at a gathering, when she picked up a spider and ushered it out the door, a friend asked, "Why bother?"

"God values all living things," Sheryl answered. "To him, an ant is as important as an elephant." Later, that friend reported back, "Because of you, I no longer squish spiders."

It may be a small thing, but Sheryl felt good that she'd made an impact. Still, few of her friends totally understood Sheryl's enthusiasm. She not only tolerated these creatures, she was fascinated by spiders, snakes, lizards, grasshoppers, and beetles. For several days, she and James had a jumping spider living in their dining room. Of course the spider wasn't shooed outside. Instead, she was welcomed, and named Gladys. Gladys sat on the dining room chair and appeared to be listening to the dinner conversation. When Gladys died, they put her in a matchbox and buried her.

Now Sheryl was ready to show the same compassion to the tarantula. She opened the car door. "I'll be right back," she said.

James smiled as she stepped out to investigate.

The tarantula was in no hurry to cross the road. The next car to come by might not be so considerate and stop. The spider, like any other creature, deserved a chance. Sheryl wasn't afraid of the tarantula; she loved every bit of it—from its eight hairy legs to its two sharp fangs. Although docile by nature, if threatened the spider might bite—and that bite could make someone sick. Sheryl, however, didn't worry. She grabbed a stick off the ground and walked over to the tarantula. She gingerly prodded the spider and scooted it across the road. Once it was safely on the other side, she got back in the car.

"Let's go," she said, now that the tarantula was well on its way.

Of course, some spiders are poisonous or dangerous. Never handle a spider if you're in doubt. The most compassionate course is to just leave it alone, and let it go on caring for its family and fulfilling its place in the ecosystem.

Most people agree that pets are part of the family. Some pets can be an important part of a family to people who don't have a home.

HOMELESS HOMER

The late fall wind whipped across the city street. Jim tugged his tattered coat tight around his neck. Underneath the coat he wore a sweatshirt, a flannel shirt, and two t-shirts. It was easier to wear them all together, since he had nowhere else to store them.

Hopefully the people filing out of the brick church across the way would take pity on him. While it was embarrassing to take handouts, that was the reality of it—he'd lost his job, his wife, and his home. He walked into the alley. Maybe he'd find something useful there. A fast food bag sat on the top of the trash can, with leftover fries. Score! Still warm, too. He hadn't eaten yet that day. He dove into the bag and raised a fry to his lips.

A whimper stopped him. He looked down. There was a small white pup with brown ears and a brown spot on its side, shivering behind the trash can. The dog sat back on his haunches and stared up at Jim with wide eyes.

Jim crouched, reached over, and gently lifted the pup. "You lost, little guy?" he asked. No collar, no tags. Skin and bones. "You're not lost. You're homeless just like me, aren't you?" He glanced at the French fries in the bag as his own stomach rumbled. The dog just stared at him without moving.

"You're probably even hungrier than me," Jim said, and handed the dog a fry. Then another. The dog ate all the fries in the bag, then looked up at Jim, licking its lips. The hunger in Jim's own belly didn't matter. For the first time in a long time, he didn't feel alone.

"I'll make you a promise," Jim said. "I don't have a lot, but I won't let you starve. I'll take care of you."

Jim tucked the pup inside his coat and wandered back to his corner. Every day he made sure Homer, as he named him, ate before he did. He found a discarded coffee mug, and filled it with water from the fountain in the town green. Whenever any money came his way, half of it (often more) went to food for his new friend. A businessman who passed by every morning sometimes handed him a small bag of kibble. Women on their way to work stopped to pat Homer and give him treats. Homer didn't have everything money could buy, but he wasn't homeless anymore either. Jim didn't keep the dog tied up. The dog never ran away.

At night they snuggled together, Homer warm inside Jim's coat. Days weren't as long, nights weren't as lonely, when they were together. Some extremely cold nights, Jim went to a shelter. He refused to stay unless they allowed Homer, too. "I don't know how long I'll be out on the streets," Jim would say. "But at least I have Homer."

One day a woman approached Jim on the sidewalk. She grabbed Homer and threatened to take him away. "You can't even take care of yourself," she said. "How can you take care of a dog?"

"No! Don't take Homer!" Jim reached for his dog. Homer couldn't be taken away. They were a team. They needed each other.

"I'm going to tell the authorities." She turned to leave, clutching the dog tightly.

"Wait a minute." The businessman who sometimes brought food was passing by. "What's the problem? I see this man every day. He takes better care of this dog than some people with all the money in the world. Look at him. Does he look mistreated to you?"

A woman stepped in. "He loves Homer. Everyone loves Homer."

Another woman stopped. "We all look out for him."

Jim's eyes welled with tears. He never knew so many people cared. The woman reluctantly returned the dog. Homer licked Jim's face happily. Jim looked at the small crowd who had gathered. "Thank you," he said. "Thank you from me and Homer."

In good times and bad, Jim had a friend to see him through. When nothing else went his way, he could always count on the love of a dog.

～

Alicia Obando, founder of the Chicago organization Pets Are Like Family, feels that when families fall on hard times, they often need a helping hand to give their pets the care they so desperately want to provide.

While working in animal rescue, Alicia saw the valuable work being done in finding homeless animals new homes, but she also ached for the families bringing their pets into the shelters because they couldn't afford to keep them. "These families already have to give up so much," she told a friend. "Giving up a pet is like giving up a member of the family."

So she started Pets Are Like Family. People in need find Alicia through contacts or by calling a hotline. After a home visit, where Alicia can see the animal and evaluate the needs, she connects families with her pet pantry, where they can obtain pet food, cat litter, leashes, and other pet care supplies. The organization also helps fund spay and neutering services, microchipping, and immunizations. "Others will tell these people who have fallen on hard times, why worry about the dog—you've got bigger problems. We honor the relationship people have with their pets. The idea of losing their pets is devastating. In times of trouble, that's when people need their pets the most," Alicia says.

A pet is happier staying where it has established bonds. It doesn't care about fancy beds and expensive toys. As long as there's no neglect or abuse, it's good for the animal to stay with the original family. It's good for the family, as well. One of the most wonderful aspects of pet parenthood is experiencing the love and compassion that only pets can give. "Owning a pet can contribute to making people more compassionate toward other people," Alicia says. "Animal lovers, in general, are more compassionate people."

I knew a kind and compassionate man, one who I knew loved animals. He also was a hunter and a fisherman, and while he never would have harmed an animal for no reason, he looked at animals in nature through a different lens than my own. It turned out that he had a serious problem with squirrels getting into the electrical wires in his home and destroying his property. He tried humane methods, including trapping and releasing them far out in the country, but that never took care of the situation. So he set out live animal traps. And there wasn't a happy ending for the captives.

One day I happened by and saw a little squirrel inside the trap. He clawed at the wire, desperate to get out. When he heard my footsteps in the leaves, he paused, looked at me with tiny, and (in my opinion) pleading, beady eyes.

Now, this wasn't my property, and it wasn't my business. That little squirrel, however, melted my heart. He didn't know any better and didn't deserve the fate that awaited him. Sure, the trap would be set again. I couldn't have saved all the bushy-tailed critters who ran about the yard. This same squirrel, in fact, may have even crept back for another peanut butter and birdseed snack. But after having looked into that squirrel's eyes, there was no way I could let him stay in the trap. I crept over and sprung the latch, and he darted away.

Now, I think I was caught springing that trap. But I hoped that the owner, knowing me the way he did, knew that there was nothing else I could do at the time. And I like to think that maybe he, too, took a little delight, as I did, in watching the squirrel bound across the yard, swishing his tail, free.

The LORD is gracious and righteous; our God is full of compassion.
PSALM 116:5

CHAPTER 7
GUIDANCE

Where you lead, I will follow

I'm not much of a hiker. While I love the country, I live in the city. Also, I have a terrible sense of direction. One of the few times I went into the woods, I got lost. I'd probably still be there now, if it weren't for an unexpected guide.

That year I'd moved to a new state. I didn't know anyone except my fiancé, Mike. I had left my job, my friends, my family. Had I done the right thing? What would my life be like now? I was a muddle of stress and worry.

One spring day I looked out the window of my small studio apartment, still a shambles of unpacked boxes. The sky was clear, the sun shone invitingly. A walk would be just what I needed to unclutter my mind. I wandered to a woodsy area nearby and followed a dirt path. I was only going to go a short distance, but the path soon became just as meandering and confusing as my worried thoughts. I'd been so preoccupied, I'd gone farther than I wanted, and I had no idea which way was out.

"Just what I needed," I sighed. If my mental deliberations weren't already muddy, they certainly were a mess now. I didn't even know where I was, much less where I was going. *God, if I'm going to get out of here, please show me the way.*

I paused to gather my wits. A little bird landed on a branch in front of me and began to sing. I spotted the bird right away, because of a flash of white on its belly. The bird cocked its head as it twittered cheerful notes. It seemed to be looking right at me. In a moment, it flew off to another branch not far ahead, looked back again, and sang. It almost seemed as if it was asking me to follow.

I stood there, having no particular idea of direction. What did I have to lose? I moved toward the little bird. As I approached, it flew off to another branch.

The beautiful bird flittered from branch to branch, with me tagging along behind. Where was it heading? The way out or deeper into the woods? Who knew? Occasionally the little sprite cocked his head and chirped.

"I'm coming, I'm coming," I said in return.

We'd traveled for a short time, when at last the bird stopped, refusing to go any farther. Great, I'd been following a bird around for nothing. Then, I caught sight of a clearing behind the trees. There was the street!

I choked out a breath of relief and picked up my pace. As I neared the clearing, the bird flitted away, back into the woods.

Was the bird just a fluke, a lucky coincidence? I didn't think so. The feathered guide was sent to lead me safely home and to remind me that God was there to look after the small stuff for me, and the bigger problems, as well, if only I had the faith to follow.

Maddison, a beautiful gray and white Great Dane, and her friend, a younger white Great Dane named Lily, were beautiful to watch together. Maddison would gently touch the younger dog with her nose. When Maddison ran, Lily ran. When Maddison paused, Lily paused. Maddison never took off without making sure that her friend was following. The older Dane patiently led the way as Lily walked beside her, nearly touching her, she was so close. The two moved as if one. To anyone observing, the two dogs were inseparable friends.

They weren't just bonded out of friendship.

Maddison was Lily's guide dog.

When Lily was a puppy, she suffered from a rare medical condition and required surgery to remove her eyes. Ever since then, Maddison stepped in to lead the way. She led Lily toward her food and water, and took her outside to play. Without her guide dog pal, Lily would have been lost and confused. Somehow Maddison knew that Lily needed her, and she appointed herself as seeing eye dog for a blind dog.

THE GUIDING SHEPHERD

There was once a police officer who noticed a German shepherd running in the road, but he at first dismissed him. Just a dog out in the night, the officer thought to himself.

He was responding to a 911 call about a house fire. The house was located in a remote area of the Alaskan woods, along winding, unmarked country roads. There were no neighbors nearby, and the nearest town was miles away. His GPS had frozen, and he'd become lost on the confusing back roads. He was about to turn when the dog ran straight toward him. Straight down the middle of the icy road.

But there was something determined about the dog's action. He looked into the officer's eyes and connected with him. Following his instincts, the officer changed directions and followed the dog.

The shepherd ran ahead in the snow, several times looking back over his shoulder and barking, making sure the vehicle was keeping up. He took several twists and turns along nearly hidden roads. He led the vehicle all the way to the raging fire. There, the officer was able to direct fire trucks and other rescue personnel, and rush to help the dog's owner, who had suffered serious burns.

There was no way the officer could have found the house on his own along the dark, confusing back roads. Thankfully, the guiding shepherd was on duty.

Roselle, a yellow Labrador guide dog, won the American Hero Dog Award for her calm and focused actions at the scene of a disaster. She led her blind partner down more than seventy flights of the World Trade Center, following the attacks of September 11, 2001. Guide dogs also help people navigate through life's milestones. A guide dog led his blind partner across the stage to receive his diploma at the University of Massachusetts, and even wore his own graduation cap and received his own diploma.

Another woman in New York found that the best guide animal for her had hooves!

PANDA AND ANN

Ann Edie walked down the street toward the school where she works, holding the handle of a leather harness. Ann is blind. Her guide animal, however, is not a dog. Ann is one of the first people to have a guide *horse*.

"Panda, forward," Ann said. The miniature horse walked ahead until she came to a curb, and then stopped. Ann moved her foot and found the curb. "Good job, Panda." Ann clicked a special training clicker and gave her horse a bite of grain.

Panda is 29 inches tall at her withers (where the back meets the shoulders) and weighs about 120 pounds. She lives with Ann and Ann's husband in their house and sleeps in a shed in the back yard. Panda runs, plays, and socializes with other horses—and she also works.

A guide horse is an uncommon service animal. Years earlier, Ann had a wonderful Labrador retriever guide dog. Bailey worked with Ann until the dog was eleven years old, which is a long time for a dog—most guide dogs retire after seven or eight years of service. After Ann lost Bailey, she heard a news report about the first blind man to use a miniature horse as a guide animal. That seemed to make sense to Ann. She had experience with horses and knew they have good vision and are calm, affectionate, and smart. And, they can live for as long as thirty years.

She called her friend Alexandra, an expert in the field of clicker training, a humane animal training method that uses clicking noises and food treats to reinforce positive behavior. "Could this work?" she asked.

"Of course," Alex answered. "Let's find you a little horse."

They found an eight-month-old black-and-white miniature horse named Panda. At first Panda lived at Alex's house learning what was called, in guide dog terms, "puppy training." Using the clicker method, Alex taught Panda to get along with people and to remain calm around loud noises. When Panda did well, she got a reward—grain, broccoli, carrots, or sometimes, her favorite—peppermints.

Panda lived with Alex for more than a year in order to learn the basic skills she needed to successfully guide Ann. Then, Alex trained Ann and Panda together, walking in different neighborhoods, her school, and shops.

When Panda came to live with Ann, the first thing she did was sniff around, then flop on her back on the carpet. Ann laughed at the sound of the horse rolling around in her living room! Of course, having a horse in the house did take some getting used to. Even though Panda was miniature for a horse, Ann still had to horse-proof her house to make sure everything went smoothly. One time Ann heard a strange *munch, munch, munch.* "Oh no! She's eating the houseplants!" Ann thought. It turned out that Ann had left a bunch of carrots on the dining room table and Panda had helped herself. Just like a new dog, Panda had to be taught not to take food from the table or counter, no matter how tempting. One thing Ann didn't have to worry about—accidents. Panda was housebroken. She could signal when she had to go out by ringing a bell on the doorknob.

Every day, Panda greets Ann with a cheerful nicker. When Ann grooms Panda, the little horse gets close and rests her nose on Ann's shoulder. When she's working, Panda guides Ann through the aisles at the grocery store, up the steps to the post office, and even onto buses and trains with an eager willingness, helping Ann maintain her independence and confidence. And every school day, Ann and Panda walk to work together.

There, Panda guides Ann to the doors and down the noisy, crowded corridors. They stop at the office, and then proceed to Ann's classroom, where Ann teaches special needs students. Panda often naps while Ann teaches. Then, at the end of the day, they walk back home together. Or sometimes after work, they go on errands, or visit the other horses at the barn. Ann removes Panda's harness and the miniature horse runs around in the riding arena. They've learned to work together, play together, and live together. They may be an unusual team, but their bond of trust and friendship gives Panda the ability to lead and Ann the trust to follow.

Not only do animals, at times, guide humans, but some animals also trust us to guide them. Gwen Cooper, author of the bestselling book *Homer's Odyssey*[7], was prepared to guide and protect her adopted blind kitten. Homer, however, surprised her with his independence.

HOMER'S WAY

"Could you take him?" the veterinarian asked. "He's a stray. Only two weeks old. He's had a nasty eye infection. Oh, and he's blind."

Talk about your hard sell.

Gwen knew that taking in a cat with special needs would be challenging. And she had her own life challenges. She'd just broken up with her fiancé, was flat broke, and was temporarily crashing in a friend's apartment. The timing couldn't be worse. Still, how could she turn the vet down? The kitten needed someone.

She brought the tiny, black shorthaired kitten to the apartment and named him Homer. He'd just had surgery to remove his eyes and was wearing an awkward plastic cone to keep him from scratching out the stitches. Gwen wrestled with questions—would he bump into furniture? How would he find the litter box on his own? How would he find his food?

She took him out of his carrier and put him right in his litter box. From there, she hoped, he could learn where other things were located in relation to the box. She watched as the kitten investigated, sniffing around the room. Amazingly, within an hour, he could locate both his litter box and his food.

To help Homer navigate, Gwen walked around the apartment. Homer used her as his "seeing-eye human," following very closely until he felt confident enough in his knowledge of the space to explore on his own. Within a day he knew his way around the whole house.

Being guardian of a blind kitten wasn't always easy, however. When little Homer climbed onto a tall chair, Gwen rushed in and pulled him down. "You're going to get hurt," she said, setting him safely on the ground. When he wedged himself into a small space, Gwen ran to his aid. She worried over his every step and hovered by his side, prepared to nudge or redirect to compensate for his blindness.

Homer, however, had other ideas. He continually ran off, confidently exploring his space. One day he climbed a high bookcase.

Gwen held her breath as Homer leapt from the shelves to a lower table. Another cat would have been intimidated to make such a leap. How had he known where he'd land? Maybe not seeing how high he was, it hadn't occurred to him that he was *too* high.

From then on, Gwen figured the best thing she could do was just stay out of his way. Homer was happiest running and playing like any other cat. Watching him climb and jump inspired her. Sometimes, she thought, you just have to take a blind leap and have enough faith in your own abilities to stick the landing. All the setbacks she faced at the moment, all the challenges in life—if Homer could face obstacles so bravely, then she could, too. It seemed as if they were guiding each other.

Had Homer come into Gwen's life at a bad time? No. Instead, the timing was perfect.

Bill Lishman, whose remarkable tale is chronicled in Columbia Picture's *Fly Away Home*, found that bonding with some birds was the key to accomplishing an inspiring flight.

THE MAN WHO FLEW WITH THE BIRDS

Bill crouched beside the nesting boxes, gazing at a brood of tiny, peeping goslings. He wanted to be sure that he was the first thing they saw. This was the key to his dream. When baby geese hatch, they imprint on, or become attached to, the first moving object they see. Bill believed that if they imprinted on him, and followed him, he could help whole populations of birds.

The dream began when Bill learned about endangered birds. One of the reasons for their loss of numbers was because, over time, some birds had lost touch with safe migratory routes. If he could teach the birds safer routes, maybe he could help restore the bird populations.

Looking over the newly hatched geese, Bill felt like a proud papa. When the goslings were ready, he took them outside and walked around the yard. Sure enough, the fluffy little birds waddled right after him. Twice a day, Papa Bill took his goslings for walks around his property.

As they grew, Bill carried his tape recorder, playing sounds of an ultralight glider. The geese followed. Later, he carried the frame of his ultralight up and down the airstrip. Again, the geese followed. But would they *fly* after him?

Finally the day came to test his plan. Bill strapped on his helmet, climbed into the ultralight, and prepared to take off. The glider rolled down the airstrip. The geese scurried out of their wire enclosure, waddling after him. He held his breath as he lifted into the air, barely daring to look back.

The ultralight glided beyond the field. Then, he heard a rustling behind him. He turned his head. The geese were following him! One by one, they had taken to the sky, hurrying to catch up with the glider.

He'd often looked up at beautiful birds in flight and imagined flying with them. Now, instead of looking up at their bellies from below, he had a stunning view. He saw the expression on their faces, the muscles moving their wings, and their chests expanding as they breathed. He felt a part of them, privileged to share the sky with these amazing creatures.

Bill's plan was successful. He and a partner formed Operation Migration, dedicated to promoting conservation of migratory species, and reintroducing endangered bird species to their native habitat. Using the same techniques as Bill had used with the geese, the team led a new generation of whooping cranes on their first migration. Once the birds knew the way, they could teach it to new generations.

Because of an amazing bond, birds allowed themselves to be guided, and ultimately saved, by a man in a glider!

When I was about eight years old, I attended a summer camp where I met a blind man with a guide dog, a beautiful young German shepherd. The dog's name was Bueno, which translated to "Good." That dog fascinated me, as I'd only known dogs as pets at the time. The man reminded me that Bueno was a working dog.

"Can I pat him?" I asked.

"Yes, but only when he isn't wearing his harness. When his harness is on, he's working. When I take it off, he can run and play as he pleases."

I watched as the man and Bueno walked down the bumpy camp path. The man let me touch the handle of the dog's harness. As I ran my hand across the smooth leather, I wondered what it would be like to have no vision.

That week in camp, I couldn't stop watching the pair. At first I felt sorry for the man in the dark sunglasses. Then I saw that he was able to do pretty much what everyone else was doing. The dog led the way. They worked perfectly together.

When I got home, I held my dog's leash and closed my eyes. Happy pulled me across the field and dragged me over a pile of rocks. I tumbled to the ground, laughing. I opened my eyes and hugged Happy tight. He wasn't trained to be a guide dog. Still, he was my best pal and I'd follow him anywhere.

Let the wise listen and add to their learning,
let the discerning get guidance.

PROVERBS 1:5

CHAPTER 8
COMFORT

Lean on me

Moses was a big, beautiful, 100-pound, cream golden retriever. He had a way of looking at you that melted your heart. He lived with our family for two weeks, long enough to make a permanent paw print on our hearts.

When we adopted Moses, we hoped he'd fit nicely into our family. Our female spaniel, Kelly, had been friends with our old yellow Lab, and we thought she'd enjoy another companion.

Unfortunately, the moment we got home it became clear that Kelly didn't like Moses. She placed herself in front of me and pounced if Moses came near. She growled and snapped, guarding her favorite bunny toy, her water bowl, and, it seemed, even the air in the room.

While we were trying to work things out between the two dogs, we took plenty of visits to my in-laws across town. My father-in-law, Ed, especially bonded with Moses. Because of his COPD, Ed couldn't get around like he used to. When he sat in his chair patting Moses, and Moses looked right into his eyes, it was easy to see that they had a special connection.

After a particularly scary doggy dispute in the kitchen, it became clear that we had to return Moses. Mike and I were devastated. We'd already grown to love Moses. Fortunately, Moses' foster mom adored the big guy, too, and decided to adopt him. We were full of remorse, and Ed especially missed the visits from his gentle friend.

That spring, Ed caught a cold and was unable to recover. After a time in the hospital, he returned home on hospice care. He slept in a hospital bed in the living room, where he could be a part of daily activities. As his illness progressed, he refused most visitors.

Mike worried. There was so little we could do to comfort his father. "Maybe we could get Moses to pay a visit," he said.

We called the foster mom who'd adopted him, and she readily agreed. "When do you want me to come?" she asked.

Mike looked at his father, breaths coming in wheezy wisps. "Better make it tomorrow," he said.

The next day Ed slept most of the morning. He hadn't the energy to eat or communicate for a few days. When Moses arrived, his new mom gave us the leash, and we led the dog over to the bedside. Moses moved gently and quietly.

"An old friend came to see you," Mike said, standing at his father's bedside. "Remember Moses?"

Ed opened his eyes. When he focused on Moses, he struggled to move. Mike extended an arm and pulled him slightly forward. Slowly, Ed stretched out his hand and touched the top of Moses' head. Just like he had all those times before. Moses sat as still as could be as Ed stroked his head and neck. For a few moments, I think, the pain and fear disappeared as Moses looked straight into Ed's eyes.

The visit lasted only a few minutes, then Ed fell right back to sleep, exhausted.

The next day Ed passed away.

I like to think that the visit gave Ed a wonderful sendoff, a beautiful reminder of the love all around him and waiting for him in heaven. Moses is a shining example of a dog who radiated that love.

Dogs often share a loving spirit, even when their own lives have been devoid of compassionate care. One young dog in Colorado had a rough start, yet still understood that everyone could use a little comfort—especially those sick and in pain.

THE CUDDLING PIT BULL

Uniformed men charged into a house in a Denver neighborhood, shouting, "Raid!"

The house had been identified as a place of dog hoarding—a situation where too many animals are kept in an unclean and unhealthy environment. A young silver pit bull shivered, but instead of running and hiding, he curled himself around the other dogs living there, mostly puppies from a different litter. He wrapped his paws over them, surrounding them like a shield.

One of the officers scooped up the silver pup and separated him from the others. "We've got to deal with this one," he ordered. "There's a ban on pit bulls in this city." Because pit bulls were deemed to be dangerous, the city had a law banning any pit bull, even if the dog had no history of aggression.

The silver dog whimpered as he was carried away, struggling to look back over his shoulder. What about the other puppies? He seemed to know they needed him.

When the eighteen-week-old pup reached the Denkai Community Veterinary Clinic in Greeley, Colorado, he cowered in the back of the carrier. A vet tech reached into his cage and lifted him onto an examining room table. The frightened pup nuzzled against her hand. There was no reason he should be banned from any place—he hadn't done anything wrong. The tech lived outside of Denver, where the municipal ordinance wasn't in affect. "I'm going to take you home," she said. She gave him a new red pillow and named him Dominic.

Dominic curled up on his pillow in his new home. Instead of the puppies he'd loved so well, he found a new friend in a little boy, the vet tech's son. Once, the tot tried to pull something off a high shelf. Dominic rushed over and herded him away so he wouldn't get hurt. One afternoon, the boy fell and bumped his head, and began wailing. Before his mother could respond, Dominic ran up and snuggled against him. The boy stopped crying.

The next time the little boy took a tumble, he ran directly to his new best friend for comfort. The two hugged and cuddled.

"You've got a gift, Dominic," the boy's mother said. And it was true.

Dominic didn't like to stay home alone during the day, so he began going to work with the vet tech. There, he rested on his red pillow. He wasn't content, however, to just lay there. When he saw an ill or injured dog, he got up and tried to follow, tripping the veterinarians and getting in the way.

"You need to stay clear," they said.

One day a dog came out of surgery, and Dominic pushed to get near him.

"No, you can't play now," the vet tech corrected.

Dominic pushed even harder. He nudged at her side and stretched his nose up to meet the sick dog. She stopped and looked into Dominic's eyes. "Are you trying to help this dog?" she asked. "Is that what you're doing?"

She set the groggy dog down on the floor. Dominic nuzzled close, wrapped his paws over him, and curled around him like a shield. The injured dog rested his chin on Dominic's front legs and closed his eyes. Dominic cuddled the dog to sleep.

"You really are amazing," she said, rubbing his head.

From then on, Dominic was given a special place outside the surgery door. He never had to be told what to do. Whenever he sensed he was needed, he lay down and waited for the patient to come out. The veterinarians focused on surgery and let Dominic take over the recovery.

The perfect job for a pit bull who just had to cuddle.

An animal's ability to make us feel calmer and happier is actually scientifically proven. When we cuddle a cat, play with a dog, watch fish in an aquarium, or pat a bunny, our level of cortisol, a hormone associated with stress, is lowered. The production of serotonin, a chemical associated with well-being, is increased. Here are some ways pets bring us comfort.

- **Improve Depression**
  It's hard to be depressed around a frisky kitten or a frolicking puppy. They love to play, and their silly antics make us laugh. They also make us feel loved. Pets accept us no matter what we weigh or what styles we wear. Pets are great listeners and never judge. Another reason pets lift depression is because taking care of a pet helps us feel needed and removes our thoughts from our own problems.

- **Ease Shyness**
  When walking alone, a shy person tends to look down and avoid contact with others. When out walking with a dog, however, more often than not, people will approach you and strike up a conversation. It's hard to avoid. And because they're interested in something you value, you don't mind talking about a pet you love.

- **Promote Calmness**
  Although pets can be rambunctious, most well-behaved pets have significant downtime. Being around a lounging pet encourages relaxation and peace. Cats are a perfect example—they sleep a lot, they are easy to care for, and their contented purring can even make us feel relaxed.

One woman even discovered that a cat can serve as a comforting counselor.

FUR THERAPY

The students gathered around the living room, standing against the wall or slouching on the couch. Niki Campbell passed around a bowl of pretzels. "Sit down, get comfortable," she said.

Niki is campus chaplain at a large engineering school. She's someone the kids can talk to when they are lonely, homesick, or worried. She often holds meetings at her apartment to give students the opportunity to get off campus and unwind.

"Does anyone have something they'd like to talk about tonight?" she asked.

The students shifted, awkward, glancing at each other with half smiles. Niki knew they were afraid to show their vulnerability. Especially Barry. He looked like he wanted to hide behind a curtain, or maybe even run out the door. Barry was from Korea and suffered from mild depression. Being in a new country created considerable pressure. Niki wondered if joining a group was overwhelming for him. She'd seen it before. The students felt stressed. Some were biomedical engineering or nuclear engineering majors, with heavy workloads. Others had problems balancing their social life with school work. Still others had questions about faith.

"Tell me about your week," she ventured, as her cat, Snickers, wove around her ankles. She stumbled over the cat as she walked around the room. How was she going to focus with Snickers in the way? She shooed her out of the room.

Niki and her husband live in a small apartment, and it isn't always easy with four cats roaming around. In addition to Snickers, who wanted to be the center of everything, there was Dave, their large Russian Blue, who was timid. Lelo, their feral rescue cat, was skittish and afraid, and gentle Dexter, their large gray tabby cat, just wanted to chill. They were each unique, just like the roomful of students.

Finally the kids began opening up. One boy talked about his family back home. As he spoke, Snickers crept back into the room and jumped on Barry's lap. Barry didn't move, but his eyes widened.

"Barry, do you want me to take Snickers away?" Niki asked.

"No, that's okay," he monotoned, glancing nervously at the calico sprawled atop his legs. Niki carried on, every once in a while peeking over at Barry. He sat stiff and still, the cat purring on his lap. After a while she noticed him gently rubbing Snickers's back. By the end of the meeting he was totally lost in her spell.

"You know," Niki said, eyeing the cat. "I bet some of you feel like Snickers here, wanting to get along with everyone. Then again, some of you might feel like our big cat, Dave, anxious around strangers and only comfortable around those he knows."

Some of the students nodded.

"Or, you might feel like Lelo, our feral cat, afraid to try new things. We have to be very gentle and take baby steps for her to come around. But you know what, Lelo trusts us more and more each day, and as she tries new things, she's starting to feel braver."

"I feel like Dexter," one of the students yawned. "Sleepy."

The others laughed. Barry hadn't shared his feelings, but he did look happier.

Two days later Niki got an e-mail from Barry. "Can I come over this week to talk?" he asked.

When Barry came over, however, he didn't have anything to say. He just sat and patted Snickers.

"I thought you wanted to talk?" Niki asked.

Barry hesitated. "Actually no," he admitted. "I really wanted to see the cat." Barry told her that patting Snickers at the meeting had left him feeling calm and happy. He realized that it worked better at easing his depression than video games, journaling, and other tactics he'd previously tried. "I wasn't sure if you'd mind," he added. "I just needed some fur therapy."

"Of course I don't mind," Niki said, smiling. *Why hadn't I thought of that before?* she wondered.

Before long, more students caught on to the idea. "Can I come over for fur therapy?" they asked.

Snickers was always happy to oblige.

Another dog, Gabriel, turned out to be an angel for stressed-out college students.

CAMPUS CANINES

Sally pulled her car into the university parking lot. Before grasping the leash of her Bernese mountain dog, Gabriel, she paused. *"God, please be with us everywhere we set our feet and paws today. Let us be a blessing and lift burdens, even if it's only for a few minutes. Let us put smiles on faces. And please open doors for me to pray for those who need it."*

Gabe was a therapy dog, and he and Sally Dick volunteered in nursing homes and hospitals. One fall day, a close family friend invited them to meet students at her college dorm. Sally had read an article claiming that students who visited therapy dogs before exams were less stressed and scored higher on their exams than the students who didn't visit dogs. Maybe this was another way Gabe could help others.

Sally expected only a handful of students. That day, more than fifty young men and women gathered around, smiling, laughing, and waiting for their turn to hug Gabriel. No more stressed-out college kids studying for exams. For a brief time, while patting Gabriel, the students were relaxed.

"I can't ignore what's happening here," the Resident Assistant said. "I'm going to make sure we schedule more of these visits, and for all the students, too!"

Each time Sally visited the college, the event grew. She needed more dogs, so she lined up ten trained therapy dogs and their handlers. Waiting for the crowd of students she knew would come, she repeated her prayer. *"Help us to reach those who need us today. Amen."*

The students arrived, running, skipping, alone or arm in arm, smiling, laughing, approaching their favorite dogs, dropping to the floor to be with them.

Gabriel loved all the attention, from the boisterous, playful students, to the more quiet, reserved ones. One such girl approached him. She fiddled with the ends of her long braids as she knelt close to Gabriel. Her sunny yellow t-shirt belied the gloominess of her expression. It was quite some time before she actually touched Gabriel. When she did, tears tumbled down her cheeks.

Sally was used to students who wanted to play with the dogs, students who liked to cuddle, even students who just wanted to talk to an adult. Often they were homesick, and the dog reminded them of a dog left behind. But sometimes, they cried.

"What's wrong?" Sally asked, stooping beside the girl with the braids.

"It's just," she sniffed, "it's just that my mom called last week, and told me that they had to put my dog to sleep. I haven't been able to think about anything else, to concentrate, to focus on exams..."

"I'm sorry. That's so hard," Sally soothed. "It's okay to cry. I still cry over dogs I lost thirty years ago."

The girl looked up. "You do?"

"Sure do." Sally asked if she wanted to talk about her dog. As the girl talked, her fingers worked their way through Gabe's thick fur. Sally didn't have to say much in response. Gabe did most of the work.

Finally the girl wiped her tears on Gabe's neck, gave him a long hug, and stood up. "I guess it's time to study for those finals," she said.

"You'll do great," Sally answered. "I'm praying for you."

The girl's eyes grew wide, as if she'd never thought a stranger would take her needs to heart. She gave Gabriel one more hug and walked away smiling.

Before they left, dozens of students had patted and hugged Gabriel. Dozens took selfies with him. Dozens wrote about him on their Facebook wall. Gabriel was tweeted, pinned, e-mailed, Instagrammed, and messaged to their friends all around the world.

After the visit, Gabe rested, sleeping off all the stress and tension he'd taken away from the students. In a few weeks, they'd do it again at another college.

Now Sally organizes therapy dog sessions at more than a half dozen local colleges and universities. Sometimes the dogs are needed during finals week, other times at Welcome Week. One time, a college student was worried about the recent increase in suicide rates and asked if the dogs could help students with depression.

"You bet!" Sally answered. And then she said her prayer again. *"God, please be with us everywhere we set our feet and paws today."*

Animals minister to people in their own homes, in hospitals, nursing facilities, and shelters; they minister to men, women, and children. Many different types of animals may be used to comfort others.

Even rats.

Yes. One Missouri woman brings her Japanese-bred domesticated white rat, Cheyenne, on visits to organizations such as

Ronald McDonald House and nursing homes. Cheyenne passed an evaluation in order to be a Pet Partner, and is comfortable being handled in public places and around noisy situations. Cheyenne wears a harness and rides in a soft cloth pouch. Cheyenne encourages people to see that rats are not disgusting, and are nothing to be feared. Most people like Cheyenne because she's small and cute, although adults are more hesitant than children to hold her. The friendly rodent offers gentle companionship and brings as much comfort to people as more popular pets.

A Pennsylvania couple implemented a similar program, bringing rescued farm animals to hospitals, nursing homes, mental health facilities, and assisted living centers. Young's Funny Farm includes ducks, a miniature horse, and even a crocodile. The animals make a strong connection with people. For some, the animals are a unique experience, having never seen or touched them before. For others, who may have grown up with pets or on a farm, the animals bring back happy memories. People can't help but laugh when they see a duck waddle down the hall, and maybe they forget about their aches and pains for a while. In addition to bringing a little joy into people's day, Young's Funny Farm provides a safe haven for homeless, abandoned, and injured animals.

In other circumstances, as when the wounds of war have taken a toll so great that normal life becomes a struggle, a furry companion can ease the pain. Amazing new programs now recognize the power of the pooch to assist veterans with post-traumatic stress disorder. Service dogs are trained to perform many tasks, such as opening doors, and retrieving dropped objects. A dog may be trained to enter a room, turn on the lights, circle the room, and come back to signal that the room is clear.

The Puppies Behind Bars program, for example, trains prison inmates to raise service dogs for wounded war veterans and explosive-detecting canines for law enforcement. A puppy grows to trust and respect a human, while helping the inmate feel valuable by nurturing a living being, who will go on in turn to help another human.

Debbie Kandoll and her Dutch shepherd Bino helped more than fifty soldiers with post-traumatic stress disorder and traumatic brain injuries. In combat, the soldiers knew someone had their back at all times. Debbie showed them that a dog could be their new combat buddy. She demonstrated maneuvers such as "Cover my Back"—Bino would move around behind her and press up against her back. When practiced with their own dog, paranoid veterans felt safe and protected. Through partnerships with trusted support dogs, these veterans became more confident and re-engaged in life. For his amazing contributions, Bino won the 2011 American Humane Association Military Hero Dog Award.

People enjoy sharing their lives with their pets, and that includes involving them in their favorite pastimes and activities. Many parks, campgrounds, stores, cafés, and hotels are pet friendly. In some cases you can bring your dog or cat on a plane or train, and many vacation resorts cater to pets by providing dog parks, activities, and even room service for dogs.

Some businesses allow you to bring your dog to work. Google, Ben & Jerry's, Clif Bar, Build-a-Bear Workshop, and Zynga are among the companies that welcome dogs. And, if your place of employment doesn't normally allow dogs, Pet Sitter International sponsors National Take Your Dog to Work Day, one day each June. Canine companions nap under desks, play in break rooms, and attend corporate meetings. In addition to bringing the joys of dogs to the workplace, the event also promotes pet adoption. Studies show that working alongside your pet actually makes you a better employee. Research by Virginia Commonwealth University found that bringing your pet to work can even lower stress and improve productivity.

THE NEW DIRECTOR OF STRESS MANAGEMENT

Another deadline. Sue Reninger took a deep breath and pushed back from her keyboard. Working as managing partner of a large advertising business in Columbus, Ohio, came with high stress, strong emotions, team and client conflicts, and the constant pressure to succeed. In the past, she would have pressed on, skipped lunch, maybe even worked all night. Not now. Not since the Director of Stress Management came on the job.

A black and white dog stirred at Sue's feet, jumped up, and pawed her leg. *Time for a walk.*

"Okay, Boone." Sue bent down and clipped on the dog's leash. She always listened to the dog's requests—after all, Boone was the new Director of Stress Management.

Sue adopted Boone from a kill shelter, just after the dog had delivered a litter of pups. Sue's heart had been aching ever since losing her beloved border collie. She hadn't been able to shake the loneliness and depression. Boone walked right up and cuddled in Sue's lap. She sensed that Sue needed her. *I'm here for you,* she seemed to say.

Taking the walk with Boone gave Sue a chance to calm down and collect her thoughts. She had a prospective new client coming in that afternoon and she needed to be prepared. They took a few laps around the building, Boone sniffing and wagging with glee, and by the time they went back inside, Sue found herself smiling.

That afternoon, the new client arrived. Sue and her colleagues walked the man into the conference room, Boone happily trotting along like she always did. Sue liked having Boone around. Her presence created a more relaxed atmosphere during what were often long and stressful meetings. Boone usually warmed right up to the clients. This time, however, when she saw the businessman, she backed away, the fur on her neck standing on end.

"Boone," Sue said, stroking the dog gently, "what's wrong?"

Boone just glared at the man and growled. As they sat around the table, Boone placed herself close to Sue's side, standing between her and the man. *Why is she acting this way?* Sue wondered.

At first Sue felt that the businessman's ideas were promising. She took notes, nodding. Then he brought up some ideas that were questionable. Unscrupulous, in fact. Then, he mentioned expecting unethical treatment in return. Sue stood up and planted her hands on her hips. "I think this meeting is over," she said.

The man grumbled, scraped back his chair, and stomped out of the room. Boone gave one last growl, then followed to make sure he went out the door.

"Good for you, Boone!" Sue praised. "You knew there was something wrong before I did!"

Boone wagged as if to say, *No problem. That's what I do!*

From then on, Sue made sure Boone was always present at meetings, including hiring new employees. If Boone didn't like someone, Sue took it seriously. Boone never again reacted to someone so strongly as that unethical businessman. And she continued giving her all to those in the office, ready to take someone out on a walk, or bring them a ball for a game of fetch, whenever they looked like they needed a little stress management.

Healing Heart Sanctuary in Southern Utah shelters and rehabilitates injured and disabled animals, while at the same time assisting children with autism, emotional problems, and other conditions. The children help feed, clean, and brush the animals. In return, the animals help the children feel needed and loved. Healing Heart Sanctuary also pairs rescued dogs from kill shelters with at-risk teens who help train the dogs and bring them to visit hospices and children's facilities, until they find their forever homes. According to the program's directors, helping an animal can be the biggest step toward helping yourself.

Dogs are used in courthouses to comfort children faced with giving testimony. The dogs sit by the child and give them a gentle nudge, encouraging them to share the details of events they couldn't face on their own. A National Institute of Health (NIH) research study found that when children are asked who they talk to when they are upset, the most common answer is their pet.

BUNNY LOVE

The big white rabbit nestled gently on the lap of a four-year-old cancer patient at the Ronald McDonald House. The little boy stroked the rabbit's soft fur repeatedly and whispered to his dad standing nearby. Wendy Mattes, the bunny's keeper and co-founder and executive director of Jasper Ridge Farm, asked the man what his son had said.

"He said he loves this bunny," the father replied gently. "The bunny knows how he feels because she's losing her hair too."

Robin is a large, white California rabbit. She has black ears, a black nose, and a black tail, and she was shedding a bit more than usual the day of the visit. Wendy had rescued the bunny from the Peninsula Humane Society and SPCA near Woodside, California. For more than a year the rabbit had waited for just the right person. Then along came Wendy, with a plan. The rabbit would join her organization and help children.

The animals at Jasper Ridge Farm provide comforting love to ill, homeless, and other children in need. Some of the animals include a beautiful pony, a cuddly guinea pig, and a funny goat. The rabbits are the most popular because they are portable, cute, and furry, and children love to hold them. The pets create calmness, decrease depression, ease loneliness, and develop a positive attitude.

One time Wendy brought Robin to visit a young boy at Ronald McDonald House who was in the Immune Wing for children with highly compromised immune systems. He was unable to go outside and touch any of the animals. Gently, she held Robin up to the window for the boy to see. The boy grinned and giggled, tension melting from his face. Just in the act of seeing the rabbit, something special transpired between the two, and for that moment his pain was eased and the little boy was comforted.

"It's the vulnerability of rabbits that children are drawn to," Wendy explains. To ensure safety, only the volunteers pick up the bunnies and put them in the children's laps. If the bunny wants to hop away, it may. Robin is nicknamed Mother Teresa because she'll patiently and lovingly sit on laps for hours. Through the gentle healing love of rabbits, special children are able to feel a little more confident and a little more secure.

All sorts of animals help to heal us, comfort us, and make us whole again. Dogs are often used to help children with attention deficit disorder, autism, and other conditions. Programs such as Library Dogs, Reading with Rover, and Tail Wagging Tutors encourage kids to read by reading aloud to dogs. Dogs are nonjudgmental listeners and are never critical when a child makes a mistake. Because the children feel comfortable, they concentrate more, their confidence soars, and their reading ability and comprehension improve.

On one occasion, a group of school children in Montana read to shelter dogs, and the benefits were entirely mutual.

BOOK BUDDIES

Grace hopped into the school van, clutching her book.

"The dogs really need you," the instructor said. "They're lonely, and they'd like to hear the sound of your voice."

Grace was a fourth grade student attending the Keystone to Discovery enrichment afterschool program in Hamilton, Montana.

Five students filled the van, heading to the Bitter Root Humane Society. They were going to help the dogs.

The program began when the director of the Humane Society called the afterschool program director, asking if they might be interested in working together. "The dogs don't get enough socialization," the director had said. "I have an idea that your kids could visit and read to them."

When the van stopped, the kids rushed into the small shelter with their books. One girl had selected a mystery book. Another chose *Bunnicula*, a funny book narrated by a dog. A boy giggled over his selection—a book about cats. Grace patted the book in her hands and headed toward a little black and white puppy. "I think she'll like this one," she said, smiling.

She sat down on a pillow next to the puppy and opened her book. "In a hole in the ground there lived a hobbit..." The pup snuggled against her side. After all the time in the shelter, in a cage, alone at night, with no family, all the young dog really wanted was someone to love. Grace rested her hand on the top of the dog's head. The puppy closed her eyes, as if the closeness gave her hope and comfort. The girl's sweet, soft voice floated over her as she read.

The program ran for six weeks. Each day, Grace rushed to the same black and white puppy to read another chapter of *The Hobbit*. The puppy jumped up to greet her, tail wagging. On the last day of the program Grace hugged the little dog tight. "I'm going to miss you," she said, her eyes brimming with tears.

That night Grace sat quietly with her mother. "That puppy is lonely. Can't we bring her home?" Her mother smiled gently and put her arm around her daughter. Grace looked up, holding her much-loved copy of *The Hobbit*. "We haven't finished the book yet."

A few days later, the family had a new member—one with black and white fur and a wagging tail. Grace's wish had come true.

They named the dog Kili, after a character in their favorite book—*The Hobbit*.

We benefit from the comfort given by cats and dogs, but animals also need our love and companionship, especially in times of difficult transition. While Sharon Azar rescued many dogs, El Duke was one of her favorites.

EL DUKE

The Manhattan apartment was cold, dark, and depressing. Mice and roaches scurried around. Worse, an old Belgian sheepdog paced the rooms, searching for his best friend.

Sharon reached out and took the dog's graying muzzle in her hand. He stood, as gentle as a deer. He looked up at her, his expression forlorn. His owner, Jose, was ninety-two and had been moved to an assisted living facility.

"They've been together for fourteen years," the social worker who stood there with Sharon said. "They were devoted to one another. Jose had even refused to go to the doctor, unwilling to leave his dog for even a few hours. Unfortunately, he suffered a stroke. That's what separated them."

Then, the landlord said the dog had to be out of the apartment, immediately.

El Duke looked so bereft. His soft eyes spoke, *Where is my person? What's happened to him?* Sharon watched him struggle to his feet. He had arthritis, two large benign tumors, and an infected eye.

"I'll find him a home," Sharon said, all the while wondering how she'd place a sickly, fourteen-year-old dog. She'd take him in, but she already had a houseful. And he'd never be able to manage the stairs. She and the social worker straightened up the apartment as best they could. Then they took El Duke for a walk in the park across the street. He wandered joylessly. Then Sharon sat beside El Duke on his blanket and called everyone she knew.

"I'll take him if you can't find anyone else," a woman named Sue said.

Despite hours of phone calls, Sue was the only one willing to foster. They met in Jose's apartment a few days later. Sue fell in love with the old dog. Their gazes met, and Sue tried to send him the message that he was safe. He rested his head in her lap and sighed. He seemed to melt with relief.

El Duke would always miss Jose, but he wouldn't be alone in his golden years. Sue would comfort him and help him get through the tough times. Sharon smiled at the quiet pair. "I'll tell Jose that his best friend will be well cared for."

One day a California businessman sought to comfort a stray cat. He didn't expect anything in return. After all, what could a tiny stray kitten do for him?

CALIFORNIA GIRL

On a Monday evening the sleek blue Miata pulled into a parking space in front of the Holiday Inn. Johnny Angell hefted his bags and traipsed toward the front door. On a temporary assignment for work, he commuted from his home in San Diego to Los Angeles every Monday, worked all week, and then returned home on Friday. He gave his all to the job, although the routine was exhausting.

As he approached the front door, he noticed the tiniest orange kitten trying to get into the hotel lobby. When she saw an opening she darted inside, only to be escorted out again and left by the curb. This happened several times as he watched. "Poor little thing," he thought. Obviously she was an unwanted guest in the hotel. The next time she was shooed away, she ran off and hid in the bushes.

That evening as Johnny looked over some paperwork, he couldn't get the kitten off his mind. The next day he drove off to the office in the morning. When he returned to the hotel that night, there was the orange kitten, sitting in his space in the parking lot, almost as if she was waiting for him.

"You can't live out here all alone. It's not safe," he said, noting the cars backing in and out and the nearby busy road. When he picked her up, she nestled into his arms. But she wasn't allowed in the hotel. "How about my car?" he asked. "I promise I'll make sure it's cool and comfortable."

First, he ran across the street to the convenience store to buy some cat food. "Should I really do this?" he wondered. He started to leave, then turned back, picked up a bag of food, a bowl, and even grabbed a free cardboard box on the way out.

He moved his car to a shady spot and opened the windows. The weather that time of year was cool and she was at no risk of overheating. He poured some food into the bowl, and she gobbled it all up. "Here's a soft towel for you to sleep on," he said. Finally, he placed the cardboard box on the floor of the clean car, hoping she'd use it for a litter box if necessary. When he opened the car door for her, she jumped in and curled up on the towel. He sat beside her and stroked her soft fur until it was time to go back to his room.

When he went back inside, he found he was much better able to concentrate on his work, and that night he slept more soundly than he had before.

The next morning he awoke early and got ready for work. He couldn't believe how eagerly he strode to his car. The pretty little kitten looked up at him and purred when he opened the door. She'd even been kind to his Miata—the makeshift litter box had been used.

The kitten lived comfortably in the car for a few days. Johnny asked around, but no one knew where the kitten belonged. He looked at her blinking eyes and hopeful expression. He just couldn't bear to put her out again and leave her all alone. "I guess you're coming home with me," he said.

The orange kitty was the perfect passenger on the drive back to San Diego. She was calm and relaxed. The only time she reacted was when a Beach Boys song came on the radio. The kitten jumped up and seemed to dance to the tune. Johnny noted the title of the song. "Well, that's it," he said. "Your name is Rhonda."

Rhonda joined the Angell family. She treated them to the most beautiful, constant purrs, a pat on their arms when she wanted attention, and a gentle, content acceptance of whatever came her way. The funny thing was that Johnny thought the rescue was to bring comfort to the little stray kitten. In reality, she was the one to comfort him.

Gabriel, the Bernese mountain dog who comforted stressed students at colleges, was also a therapy dog, visiting hospitals and nursing homes. He walked into my life one day. When my husband was sick in the hospital, I didn't know where to turn for comfort. I huddled in the vinyl chair near the foot of the hospital bed. That man lying there, pale and still, monitors blinking all around him, oxygen tube clamped to his nose—I barely recognized him. How could that be Mike, the husband I'd relied on for thirty-one years?

My take-charge guy was battling multiple blood clots in his lungs that had debilitated his body. The doctor said the worst was over. Now we just had to be patient. But I'd made myself sick with worry, spending my days at the hospital and night after sleepless night at home, scared and completely on my own. For the first time in my life, I had no one to depend upon.

We were one of those couples who did everything together. At breakfast we did the daily crossword puzzle, sharing a pen. We went together to the gym, where we climbed aboard adjacent treadmill machines, plugged in our ear buds and watched the same show on TV. When Mike tapped me on the shoulder and pointed to the screen, I always knew exactly what he was thinking.

Mike was my rock. *Lord, please help him get better. I feel all alone without him.* A strange sound came from the hospital corridor. A sharp *click-click-click-click* on the linoleum floor drew nearer till it stopped outside Mike's room. I did a double take. A dog loomed in the doorway.

I recognized the breed by his distinctive black and white coat highlighted by rust-colored markings—a Bernese mountain dog. A special collar distinguished him as a therapy dog. I gazed at Mike, awake but dazed.

I'd been a dog lover all my life, but what could a therapy dog possibly do to help my husband? The dog seemed to read my thoughts. The dog had a job to do and he got to it. Purposefully, he stepped into the room, handler in tow. I sat quietly watching this well-trained beauty. Maybe petting the dog's soft fur would give Mike some small comfort.

As the dog headed toward Mike's bedside, however, he suddenly stopped. He turned and padded over to my chair and looked into my eyes. With that, the dog nudged his head against my waist, as if asking for a hug. I put my arms around him and buried my face in his thick, velvety fur, until I felt the gentle pulsing of his heart.

I am here, its rhythm seemed to say.

My whole body relaxed. My stress lifted away. Mike smiled from the bed. The dog let me hold him for as long as I needed to. When I finally released him, he put his paw on my knee and looked up at me.

I turned to his handler. "How did he know that I was the one who needed him?"

"Gabriel always knows," she said.

I stroked the dog's neck. Gabriel. My angel dog. The Lord knew how to soothe me. He'd keep me strong while my husband regained his health. On that I could depend.

Even though I walk through the darkest valley, I will fear no evil, for you are with me; your rod and your staff, they comfort me.

CHAPTER 9
FAITHFULNESS

Always by my side

Moses was rarely without his worn, red leash.
The big golden retriever would drag it around inside and outside
of our house. He'd lie under our dining room table, leash between
his paws. The leash was all he had left from his previous life.

We shared our home with Moses for only a short time before
he went on to his real forever home, but he made a huge impact
on our lives. I think it was especially because of his story and his
faithfulness to his former owner.

Moses had lived with a family in the suburbs until the parents
divorced, and the father took him to a secluded mountain cabin.
There, the man became somewhat of a hermit, preferring to spend
his time alone with his dog. One of the few times they left the
cabin was on Sunday mornings, to go to church. I'm not sure where
they worshipped, or whether the dog went inside or waited outside, but they went to church together.

I got the impression that the man and dog did everything together. They must have gone on many long walks together, as much as Moses loved his red leash.

Sadly, one day the owner passed away. He lay there in his cabin for more than a week before he was discovered. The whole time, Moses waited by his side. I can only imagine how he felt, unable to rouse the man, probably nudging him and licking his face, maybe fetching his leash and begging his best friend to go for a walk.

When Moses came to our home, he walked around, a bit dazed. There were new surroundings, new people, other dogs to get used to. When he got overwhelmed, he'd find his leash and a quiet corner. He often closed his eyes and drifted off to sleep. Holding that red leash in his mouth, I know he felt connected to the man he loved so well, the one he stayed by, faithfully, until the man's very last day, and beyond.

The profundity of a dog's faithfulness is illustrated in two classic stories. The first dates back to the 1800s in Scotland when a little Skye terrier named Bobby belonged to a night watchman named John Gray. They made their rounds together, the little dog faithfully trotting at his master's side. Eventually, Gray developed tuberculosis. When he died, he was buried in a cemetery called Greyfriar's Kirk.

While several versions of the story exist, the most popular version recounts that the little dog mourned his master at the funeral, and chose to stay there afterward, close to the man he loved. Even attempts by the cemetery groundskeeper to shoo him away didn't work. The lonely dog wouldn't budge.

Bobby lay on his owner's grave every day for fourteen years.

The stone marker near the grave reads, "With such sacrifice, God is well pleased."

The second story is about Hachiko, the now-famous Akita, who also refused to give up on his caretaker and best friend. His story took place in the 1920s, in Japan. Hachiko's owner was a professor at the University of Tokyo. Every morning, Hachiko strolled along with Professor Ueno to the train station and watched him board the train for work. Later that evening, Hachiko was right there outside the station, waiting for his friend to return.

One day, Hachiko waited, but his friend didn't get off the train. Tragically, the professor had died unexpectedly while at work. No one could explain that to the dog. Hachiko sat waiting at the train station, staring at the place from which his best friend reliably emerged. Hours ticked by. The dog eventually went home and rested, but the next evening, at precisely the time the train was due, he returned to the station and sat in his usual spot, gazing at the station door.

Every day, at exactly the same time, Hachiko returned to the train station, waiting for his master to return, for more than nine years.

Hachiko's story became so popular that, during a visit to Japan, Helen Keller commented that she'd like to have an Akita for a pet. She was given one as a gift, and is credited with popularizing the breed in the United States.

In Texas, another faithful dog revealed his heartache and his undying love.

PICTURE PERFECT

The house suddenly seemed too big. Everything seemed empty, too quiet. Nancy Robinson passed by the open bedroom door and stopped suddenly at the sight of her three-year-old huskie mix, Co-Coa. What she saw nearly broke her heart.

Six months earlier, Nancy's forty-four-year-old husband had passed away unexpectedly of a heart attack. The last thing he'd done that tragic day was to give Co-Coa a bath.

Nancy remembered the day they'd brought home the tiny pup with huge feet. He loved her, but he *adored* her husband. Co-Coa was his hiking pal. His fishing buddy. They went everywhere together.

Then came that terrible day. She had to pry Co-Coa away to give the paramedics room. Since then, Co-Coa sulked. Nancy was still dealing with her own grief. How could she help their dog?

That's when she saw Co-Coa in the bedroom. He was sitting on the bed, staring at a picture of her husband that hung on the wall. He stared so intently, he didn't notice Nancy tiptoe into the room. She'd never known a dog to pay particular attention to a picture before, but Co-Coa was focused, centered. The dog's expression was so serious, his eyes sad and questioning. *What happened?* they seemed to ask. *Where is he?*

Nancy sat on the bed beside Co-Coa and slipped her arm around his shoulders. "He didn't want to leave you," she said. "He'll always love you." Co-Coa sank into her embrace. In her time of need, she felt comfort in sharing the mourning. Her dog's love for her husband endured, even after he was gone.

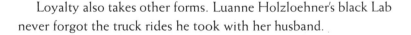

Loyalty also takes other forms. Luanne Holzloehner's black Lab never forgot the truck rides he took with her husband.

IN THE DRIVER'S SEAT

More than anything, Topper the black Lab loved to ride in the big, white Silverado truck. Topper lived with Henry and Luanne and a collection of other animals on a little farm in Vermont. Henry used the truck to do all his errands. Topper never wanted to be left behind. Most of the day he lay around, fat and lazy, but when he heard Henry pick up the keys and open the front door, he shot out and beat Henry to the truck nine times out of ten.

Topper rode around in that truck, big blocky head out the window, tongue lolling in the breeze. It was as if he never wanted to be without his buddy. As he drove, Henry reached over and scratched the dog's side. Henry wasn't much of a talker, but that was okay. All Topper cared about was just being by his side. When they stopped at the General Store, he leapt out and followed Henry around as he picked up groceries and animal feed. He wouldn't let Henry out of his sight—no chance risking he'd get away without Topper there, riding shotgun.

Sadly, after ten years together, Henry passed away from cancer. Luanne did her best to pick up the pieces, including comforting the old dog as he paced around the house as if lost. She sat beside Topper and rubbed his ears. "You miss your buddy, don't you?" It wasn't easy, however, to make him feel better when she was still reeling herself.

About a week after Henry passed away, Luanne lent the truck to a friend who had a heavy load to haul. One day the truck rumbled back up the long, dirt driveway. Topper's ears perked. He lifted his head from the rug and listed to the familiar engine noises. Excitedly, he jumped up and bolted toward the door. When Luanne opened it, he raced to the truck, joyfully wagging.

"Well, hello there," the man who had borrowed the truck said.

Topper stopped wagging, sunk back on his haunches, and hung his head.

"I'm sorry." Luanne bent down and hugged the forlorn dog, her eyes brimming. "It's not him. I'm sorry. I'm sorry." Her wet cheek brushed against the dog's soft fur.

Several weeks later, Luanne decided to sell the truck. It was too big for her to drive. As the new owners came to pick it up, Topper jumped in the open door and sat fast in the driver's seat. It was as if he couldn't bear to let the truck go.

Although his best friend was gone, he never forgot the joyful rides they took together.

In 2013, a neuroscientist searched for scientific evidence to support the idea that dogs have the capacity to experience human emotions. He trained dogs to enter an MRI scanner, which measured brain responses to certain hand signals and smells. Based on maps of the dogs' brain activity, the scientist concluded that dogs have the same capacity to experience emotions, such as love and attachment, as human children. So, while some think that dogs hang around us simply because we feed them, this study suggests that dogs are faithful because they love. The deep bonds of faithfulness are not only possible, they are a wonderful part of what makes us love animals, and animals love us in return.

An insightful photographer captured a moment of pure love and devotion between a Wisconsin man and his faithful dog.

THROUGH THE LENS

The man stood in the deep, brisk waters of Lake Superior, cradling his dog, the dog's head tucked neatly under his chin. Hannah Hudson lay on the dock, stomach pressed to the wood, facing the water, camera poised. The moment was right. She clicked the shutter and with a snap took the picture of John Unger and his dog Schoep that the world would come to love.

Hannah had met John in passing a few years earlier. She met Schoep on her daily dog walks with her retriever and her Chihuahua. Schoep was in his yard, and Hannah stopped and scratched his ears and rubbed his neck. This was an old dog—very old, by the looks of him. Gazing into Schoep's graying face, she felt drawn to his noble beauty. He reminded her of her previous dog, which had lived to be eighteen years old. There was something deep and wonderful about an old dog.

The next time she saw John, she'd told him that, if he was interested, she'd be willing to take pictures of his dog. Hannah is a professional photographer who travels throughout the country taking quality pictures of pets and shelter dogs, and also holds workshops to teach shelter employees how to take better images of their dogs, to help them get adopted.

A short time later she received a phone call, asking if she could go to the lake for the photo shoot.

That day had been particularly busy, and Hannah had only a brief window of opportunity, but she wasn't going to let down her friend. She grabbed her equipment and rushed to the lake.

When she arrived, she spotted the two out in about four feet of water. Schoep was nineteen and suffered from arthritis and hip problems that made walking painful. John took him into the lake as a way to relieve the pressure and soothe the dog's joints. John was leaning, the large dog heavy in his arms. His long hair, tied back in a ponytail, dipped into the water. Schoep was partially submerged, his muzzle resting on John's chest. As the water surrounded him, the old dog began to relax. John embraced the dog under his front legs, as the rest of him floated. Schoep closed his eyes, his head against John's chest. Before long, he fell asleep.

Knowing the right shot is instinctual for a good photographer. She dismissed shooting from the beach and focusing on John, but ran onto the dock to get eye level with Schoep. She wanted to see the bond, to see Schoep feeling comfortable. The dog's expression was peaceful, his eyes lightly closed, his mouth curved up in a bliss-ful smile. What she saw in that moment, and hoped to capture, was a dog that completely trusted his owner.

Everything came together: the old dog, the candid moment, things moving quickly. She took a few shots, and then had to get up and rush off to her next appointment.

When she finally got a chance to look at the photo, she was pleased. In that moment she'd captured, Schoep felt no pain; he was at peace in the arms of the man he loved. She liked the image and put it up on her website and Facebook page. She was totally unprepared for the response.

The photo went viral, with millions of views and shares. The devotion between John and his dog touched everyone's heart. Hannah's skill as a photographer is only half the explanation. Her love and devotion to her own dogs enabled her to see an inspirational connection between another human and his dog. In a click of the lens, she captured an expression of compassion and devotion that every human should offer and every animal deserves.

Because of this great faithfulness, some people will give up everything to help animals in need.

A GREATER CALLING

Commuting to her law office in Blue Springs, Missouri, Dana Apple once noticed something lying in the grassy median. "Oh no," she thought. "An animal's been hit by a car."

The animal, now more clearly a large, black dog, raised its head. It was alive.

Wanting to help, Dana stopped. She turned her truck around, grabbed a rope out of the back, and called the emergency number for assistance.

With cars speeding down I-70, Dana made her way across the two-lane highway. Even while dodging traffic, she prayed not for herself but for the animal laying in the grass. "Please let it be all right," she whispered.

About the time she reached the median, the emergency responder arrived. Together, they secured the dog and led it to Dana's truck. The dog was far along in pregnancy.

Instead of heading to work that day, Dana drove directly to the vet's office.

The docile dog wagged as if nothing was wrong. She wore no collar, and scans showed no identifying microchip. "Has she been hit by a car?" Dana asked as the vet performed his examination.

"It doesn't appear so," the vet answered. "She must have been on her own for such a long time to be in such bad shape. She's weak and emaciated but otherwise, no injuries…just pregnant."

"How soon?"

The vet smiled. "Any time now."

At home, Dana settled the exhausted dog she named Lillian onto some blankets in a quiet room. Since she hadn't been hit by a car, Dana figured she'd just lain down in the road and didn't have the energy to get back up.

The next morning when Dana checked on Lillian, the first puppy was being born.

She called her office. "I'm not going to make it to work today, either."

The delivery, however, didn't go well. Dana packed up Lillian and the first puppy and rushed them to the vet's office. There, six more puppies were delivered by caesarian section. They all survived! Dana cheered when she got the news. But as Dana rejoiced, the vet handed her the bill and the box of helpless pups.

For the first time, reality hit her. "These are mine?"

The vet nodded.

What was she going to do with eight dogs? She had commitments. A demanding job. Other animals to care for. The dog wasn't even hers! But she looked at Lillian, her sweet face so trusting, her tail still wagging. Lillian and her puppies deserved a chance.

The next day Dana bought lumber and built a 10'x10' pen, and added soft blankets. "I'll be in next week," she told her law partner.

Lillian needed help—she tried to be a good mother, but she was so weak and had been malnourished, that she couldn't produce enough milk. Dana spent $20 a day on puppy formula. She sat cross-legged in the pen with the new family and a bottle. Lillian rested her head in Dana's lap as the babies were fed. Dana sang to her. Lillian closed her eyes and relaxed. When the puppies were restless, she sang to them too. "Amazing Grace, how sweet the sound," she sang. She especially liked the line about "once was lost, but now I'm found." Where would Lillian and the puppies be now, if she hadn't found them?

Feeding so many hungry mouths took well over an hour. Then in no time at all, they were whining for more. Dana fed the puppies every three hours. Night and day. She didn't miss a feeding. She didn't call in reinforcements to help. The pups were her responsibility and she was going to see to it that they were well-nourished and got the start to life they deserved.

There were times she curled up with the pups, exhausted. Their care was demanding. Then, Lillian would look up at her with love in her eyes. Even though she was missing work and losing money, Dana knew she was doing the right thing.

Lillian grew healthy and the puppies grew fat. Dana found good homes for five of the pups. She kept two and, of course, Lillian. In all, Dana missed a month of work. But the hungry, exhausted dog who was once too weak to move had someone to love her, to nurture her babies, and to give her a home. She once was lost, but now was found.

Years ago, when my kids were young, we gathered to say goodbye to a faithful friend. My nine-year-old daughter moved a fat black marker across a pink paper. My six-year-old son held a crayon, his freckled face solemn.

"What do you want to say?" I asked.

"You were a good dog," he replied.

"Okay," I answered. "Write it down here." Carefully, he formed the letters onto the paper with his crayon. "And, I'll miss you," he added.

"That's good," I said. "Schuyler will like that."

Schuyler, our dalmatian, had lovingly welcomed both of our children into the family. He'd grown to become our kids' best friend. I remembered when he'd watched our daughter in her infant swing, gently touching his nose to her feet as she moved forward. Or how he sat underneath our son's highchair, catching the Cheerios that tumbled over the sides. Or as the kids grew older, how he ran in the yard with them and romped in the fallen leaves. Now he was gone. The vet had discovered a tumor. We were devastated. And, for the first time in their lives, our kids experienced loss.

The sun was fading under the distant hills. We talked about how much we loved Schuyler and how he'd be missed.

"When Schuyler reads these letters in heaven, will he remember us?" my daughter asked.

"Of course he will," I answered, pulling them close. "And we'll never forget Schuyler." We would remain as faithful to our dog's memory as he'd always been faithful to us.

Great is Thy faithfulness.

LAMENTATIONS 3:23 KJV

CHAPTER 10
LOVE

The greatest gift of all

Who'd have thought the words would have

come out of my mouth: "Whatever you do, don't get that dog!"

I love dogs! There's never been a time in my life I haven't shared my home with at least one canine companion. But the pooch my husband Mike was gaga over on the pet rescue group's website was absolutely the wrong dog. And this was definitely the wrong time.

Mike had just been released from a lengthy hospital stay with a serious condition. Blood clots lodged in his pulmonary artery had almost taken his life. I finally got him home and couldn't stop worrying about his condition. He was weak and needed his rest. Instead, he spent all his time staring at a website, pining away for a dog.

An old dog.

I leaned over his shoulder and snuck a peek at the screen. The large retriever's golden fur looked like it had been shaved, probably due to matting or allergies. His long limbs appeared knobby and wobbly. His teeth were crooked. His sad eyes told me that he'd been through a lot. His expression was deep. Pleading. Irresistible. But, no! His age! The website stated that he was eleven. I'd never had a dog live past twelve years old. I wanted to help him almost as much as Mike wanted to help him. Then I got practical. Old dogs were more likely to have issues with their health. Brittle hips and bones. Respiratory and digestive issues. Cataracts. I already had Mike's health to worry about. Although we weren't senior citizens yet, it wasn't *that* far off.

I turned away from the computer. "I'll get your medicine, honey."

While Mike took his pills, his focus remained on the screen. "Let's just go look at him," he said hopefully. "Just to see."

When had I ever been able to "just look" at a dog and not want to take it home? Mike knew me well. How could he not after thirty years of marriage?

Then he locked me in his gaze and delivered the crushing blow. "Honey, he needs us."

The next day Mike arranged for us to meet the rescue worker in the parking lot of a nearby pet food store. He beamed as we left the house, his step livelier than I'd seen in weeks. My step lagged.

"Let's hurry before someone else claims him!" he said.

Not likely. Slim chance anyone would jump to adopt an eleven-year-old dog. Puppies went fast. Not so for older dogs.

When we arrived, the rescue worker opened her car door. Out crept a lanky, old golden retriever. He stood stock still, as if waiting for permission to move ahead. "He was abandoned, so we have no idea of his past, where he lived, medical records."

His coat was dull and patchy. His ribs stuck out. He averted his eyes, and I wondered if he was even capable of making a connection. *He needs a home, to be sure, but we aren't the right home.* I stooped low and he slowly turned his head toward me. When I touched him, he didn't budge, as if he'd lost all hope. Then I noticed his tail. A tiny movement, a hesitant wag. There was some hope, yet.

"He'd been on his own for quite a while," the rescue lady explained. "Probably was dumped by the roadside. Then passed around to shelters and rescue groups for more than a year."

Abandoned. Homeless. Unwanted. My heart lurched. I reached down and surrounded his neck with my arms. "Poor boy. Sweet, sweet boy." This time he moved. He leaned into my touch. His muscles relaxed against me. It felt as if he melted, fully trusting to become one with me.

My heart melted, too.

I glanced at Mike. He was a goner, his eyes as pleading as the dog's.

I whispered. "But . . . he's eleven, remember?"

Mike put his hand in mine. "Doesn't he deserve a nice home and some happiness in his golden years?"

I stroked the dog's head again. When I stopped, he pushed his nose into my palm, asking for more. Mike was right. Even though I wasn't sure about adopting an old dog, I couldn't say no.

When we got home, we introduced our new friend to our spaniel, Kelly. She wasn't thrilled, but she accepted him from a distance. We'd work on that.

We named him Brooks. That afternoon Mike and Brooks relaxed together, Mike in the old recliner chair, Brooks on the floor at his feet. Later, they took a walk. "Not too fast," I called. Turns out there was no need to worry—Brooks and Mike had about the same pace.

In the evening, Mike stood at the kitchen shelf, preparing his medications. Brooks needed steroids for a skin condition. "Come on," Mike called cheerfully, "us old men have to take our medicine." Brooks trotted up and took the medicine right out of Mike's hand. Mike leaned over and kissed him on the nose.

Every day I watched Brooks transform from a scrawny, with-drawn, abandoned dog to a healthy, happy golden with a heart full of love. At the same time, my husband was transforming. No longer focused on his health and his limitations, instead his attention turned to caring for Brooks. When Mike rested in his chair, Brooks curled up on top of his feet. He followed Mike from room to room, and lay down by the door to wait for him if he went out. Even though the old dog had been abandoned and unwanted, he had a heart full of love. A love that helped him heal and helped Mike heal as well.

Watching Mike and Brooks together, the heavy grip of worry that surrounded me began to fade. Life isn't just about an age, or being healthy or sick. It's about trusting God with all of it and living fully.

In the evening I heard Mike call to Brooks again, "Time for us old men to take our medicine."

I went to Mike and gave him a hug. Then I hugged Brooks. He softened against my side, fully trusting. Fully loving.

Brooks lived with us for about a year, until cancer took his life. He was a beautiful example of unconditional love. To me, this means that dogs have a capacity to love fully, even if the world has treated them unjustly.

Can wild animals show love? Do animals love each other? Aline Alexander Newman, author of *National Geographic's Ape Escapes, Animal Superstars*, and other animal books, says, "Love is hard to define, because it means different things to different people." Usually, we identify human love by asking people how they feel.

"But animals can't talk. So some scientists say we can't know what they're feeling, or design experiments that will tell us. While it's true that anecdotes can't be replicated, if we gather enough of them, don't they add up to data? Otherwise, what are we to make of true stories like these: a mother elephant plunged into a raging torrent to lift her baby to safety. A grizzly bear caught salmon and fed her injured brother for weeks, until he healed enough to care for himself. And a father tiger took over the raising of his two cubs after their mother died. He did this in spite of the fact that male tigers normally do nothing to raise their young—and sometimes even kill them! If humans did these things, we'd call it love. So let's call it love in animals, too."

Animals form strong attachments to people, too. And for pet parents, this is clearly love. Animals show us love in many ways. A wag of the tail. A kiss. Or perhaps, a dance.

DO YOU WANT TO DANCE?

"Did I do the right thing?" Dawn Miklich thought for the hundredth time. The small African grey parrot she rescued thrashed in its cage, shrieking hysterically.

Kijivu, which means "gray" in Swahili, had been unhappy in his former home. Something there had frightened him. Not knowing what to do to help Kijivu, the inexperienced family had progressively made things worse. Dawn thought she could give him a better life. Apparently not. Kijivu hadn't shown much sign of adjusting. He squawked and flapped his wings frantically whenever she came near. It was as if he couldn't accept that she was there to help him. In the worst times, he flapped so much that he tumbled off his perch, feathers flying, broken in the fall. "It's okay, I'm not going to hurt you," she'd say, shaking her head sadly.

Maybe this wasn't the right home, she worried. She almost felt like he didn't like her. Maybe the best thing was to find him a new home, with people who didn't make him afraid.

She looked at his bright eyes and inquisitive expression. He was intelligent. Despite his fears, his vocabulary expanded every day. He listened to her from the other room and repeated words she said. No, she just couldn't give up on him. She had to try.

It took four months for Kijivu to stop flapping and thrashing every time she walked in the room.

"Maybe he's starting to trust me," she thought.

After eight months, he hesitantly snatched a treat from her hand. Slow progress, but progress nevertheless. Eventually, he let her sit near the cage in a darkened room. She talked to him, bobbing her head to imitate his dance. She did this every day. Kijivu observed quietly.

Early one morning, after a year of trying to get the parrot to feel comfortable with her presence, Dawn crept into the room and sat close to the cage. A dim light shone in from the hall. Kijivu inched close to where she sat.

"Hello," she said. "Good morning, Kijivu."

The parrot cocked his head. His bright eyes shone. Then he started chattering, a happy sound. Dawn grinned. Maybe he recognized her as someone who loved and cared for him. She bobbed her head. "Do you want to dance, Kijivu?"

Kijivu whistled. Then he started bobbing his head, too, mimicking her movements. With no sign of fear, he swayed, close to the side of the cage near where she sat. A joyful lightness lifted her spirits. Then suddenly Kijivu stopped moving. She frowned. Was he okay? Was it too much, too fast?

Kijivu cocked his head. "You're silly," he said.

Dawn burst out laughing. "You're silly, too, Kijivu!" she said.

And together, they danced.

While Bulldog's heart was as big as all of Texas, after he passed away Sam Adams struggled to find room in his own heart for another dog.

THE PERFECT DOG

There was no other dog like Bulldog. A special gift, given by God. The boxer had been loving and devoted, following Sam around the cattle farm. He was forgiving, too, licking the hand of his former abuser. He was, in a word, perfect.

When Bulldog passed away, Sam couldn't get over his grief. He'd lost a true friend. Everything Sam had given, Bulldog doubled and tripled in return. Still, Sam longed for another boxer in his life. A dog to follow him around the farm. A dog to share the closeness and love that he was privileged to share with Bulldog.

So Sam searched. Finding a new boxer didn't turn out to be easy. After months, Sam wondered if there was a dog out there for him. One evening he dropped to his knees. "God, through my own efforts I am failing. I can't do it myself. But I know you know the right dog. Please, God, find me a friend who needs a friend." God would provide that which his heart so missed.

The answer still didn't come.

Then, after a year, Sam spied an ad in the paper. "Tyson, 4-year-old boxer, is in need of a forever home. If not adopted he will have to go to a shelter."

Sam rushed out a reply. "My wife and I are in our late forties. We live on a 300-acre cattle farm. Our house is a good quarter mile off of the highway and a dog can play safely in our yard. I have had boxers all of my life and most recently lost my dear boy, Bulldog. I didn't rescue him, he rescued me." There was a lump in his throat as he wrote.

Sam put off meeting Tyson for two weeks He was too afraid to give his heart again, but wanted to all at the same time. His heart won. He went and picked up Tyson.

Sam didn't know right away if Tyson was the perfect dog. Sure, he had perfect manners. He was obedient and friendly. But the ache in his heart didn't go away.

Then one day Tyson ran up and gave Sam a silly look, tongue lolling to the side, ears pert, and bowed low like he wanted to play. Of course he did! As they ran and tumbled, Sam felt lighter than he had in months. Happy. It was that day that he and Tyson entered each other's hearts.

Tyson became Sam's constant companion. Like Bulldog, he followed him around the farm and never let him out of his sight. He fit into every aspect of Sam's life.

Early one morning Tyson jumped on the bed. Sam scratched his ears. "Bulldog would be happy that you take such good care of me," he said. The joy on the dog's face was as much of a good morning greeting as anyone could ever want.

Sam wouldn't, couldn't get over Bulldog—that boxer would always be a part of him. But there was a way to ease the grief. In all the time of looking and longing, Sam knows that his search had been directed. "Thank you for Tyson, and for uniting us," Sam prays every night.

God had found the perfect dog and sent him to Sam.

Can animals form strong, loving friendships? You might want to ask Mario the goose.

BEST FRIENDS

Echo Park in California is a beautiful environment for geese. Plenty of water, enough plants and bugs to eat, and other geese for companionship. One particular goose, however, didn't want to hang around with others of his species. Mario chose his own companion, and his best friend had two legs, gray hair, and a little red scooter.

Dominic Ehrler rode to the park on his scooter every day. Retired, he enjoyed the exercise, fresh air, and leisurely strolls along the paths. The minute Mario got a *gander* at Dominic, he followed. Maybe he liked the way Dominic walked. Maybe he liked the food in his pocket, although lots of people fed the geese. No, it was more than that. Mario chose Dominic to be his best friend.

Mario stayed at a distance at first, tagging along like a shadow. Then he got close enough for Dominic to reach out and touch him. He didn't normally like when people tried to touch him, but Dominic was special. Before long, Mario proudly waddled along beside Dominic as he walked. Together, they strolled all the way around the pond. If other people got too close, he hissed and snapped at them. Dominic was *his* friend.

Each day, the moment Mario spotted Dominic's red scooter, he wiggled all over and skedaddled out of the pond. Then, they spent hours together, walking around the pond. When it was time for Dominic to leave, Mario honked loudly and flapped his wings. As Dominic rode away, he ran beside him, his webbed feet hitting the pavement, until, flapping his wings mightily, he lifted into the air. He flew low beside the red scooter, just over Dominic's shoulder as he drove down the road. If he had it his way, he'd follow him all the way home.

Dominic always circled back to the park and waited, often until the goose fell asleep and he could sneak off. "I'll be back again tomorrow," he'd say. Because that's how it is between best friends.

In an Associated Press–Petside.com poll, half of Americans responded that they consider their pets part of the family. Seventy percent of pet owners say they sometimes allow pets to sleep on their bed; 65 percent buy Christmas gifts for their pets; 23 percent cook special meals for their pets; and even 40 percent of married women with pets say they get more emotional support from their pets than from their husbands!

We show our love for our animals by sharing our homes and making them a part of our family. By protecting their environments. By treating them humanely. God created animals on earth and commanded us to take care of them.

Sometimes loving a dog means helping them over the rough patches, so that the dog can offer all the love it has to give.

FOR THE LOVE OF SIS

Sissy the greyhound went willingly into her crate at the adoption center. When the long, lean length of Sis was inside, the volunteer closed the door. Then Sissy lay down on her cushion, curled pretzel-tight with her tawny back pressed against wire, and tucked her nose under her paw. She faced the wall, away from Shawnelle Eliasen and her family.

"I don't think this one likes people," the teenage son, Grant, said.

Shawnelle pushed her hands into her pockets. "Sissy? Look here, girl. Sweet girl, hello."

Sissy didn't move.

"I'm not sure we want a dog who doesn't like us," Grant said. They moved down the row and looked at a different dog, a cinnamon-colored little greyhound with a broken leg. She stood, despite a cast, and looked Grant in the eye. Her tail wagged like mad.

Shawnelle half-wondered if her son was right. They had a big family—herself, her husband, and five boys. Why would she consider adopting a dog who just wanted to be left alone?

Shawnelle glanced back at Sis. The answer came quickly—it was because of her eyes. Shawnelle had gazed into the eyes of dozens of lovely dogs—white, brindle, brown, black, and fawn colored. They all had different personalities, just like people. Many of the greyhounds they'd spent time with in the visiting room and in the play yard were much more affectionate and friendlier than Sis. But Sissy's eyes were the deepest brown she'd ever seen. Big, wide, almond-like. They seemed like a reservoir, holding something deep and precious. Sis, she knew in her heart, had a capacity to love.

Several more times before the decision was made, the family visited Sissy. Shawnelle bypassed the friendly pick-me dogs until she reached the solemn Sis. Six-year-old Gabriel made it a mission to get her to take a treat from his hand. She'd duck her head, as if ashamed. When he set the treat on the ground, she'd hesitate, and then slowly take it.

"She'll do it, Mama," he said wide green eyes hopeful. "She's scared. She needs to know that we're safe."

One day they were running with Sis on the dirt-packed yard at the shelter. She'd been an average racer—Shawnelle had watched her contests online. But when she took long figure-eights around the yard, moving in the way God made her to move, she was beautiful and graceful. When the volunteer called from the door, Sis stopped. But she didn't run to the volunteer to go back into the safety of her crate. Instead, she leaned into Shawnelle.

"I guess she's your girl now," the volunteer said.

Shawnelle sat on the ground and took Sis's long face in her hands. "Are you, girl? Ready to be mine?"

They brought Sis home the next week. Sissy hadn't been inside a house before. Everything was new. Windows. Stairs. Music. Dishwasher. Vacuum. Tile floors. The sounds of a household of children. If it wasn't present at the track or the breeders they'd been told, a greyhound wouldn't know how to respond. If they moved suddenly, or something fell off a counter, she bolted away. Trash bags scared her to death. Someone had to remove Sissy from the kitchen while another took out the trash.

At first, Sis spent a lot of time in her crate, with the door open so she could come and go as she pleased. When she came out, she was met with a barrage of little boys.

"We need to be gentle with her," Gabe said over and over. "She's four, but she's like a baby."

Four-year-old Isaiah would gently stroke her fur. "You have a home, Sissy," he said.

Samuel, their ten-year-old, was patient and kind. "It's okay, girl. You'll never have to be sad. You have us now."

Sissy would tolerate the attention for a few minutes, then she'd hang her head and return to her crate.

Shawnelle found herself staring at Sissy, wondering what her life experiences had been. Greyhounds have strong memories. Were Sissy's sad? Had she felt threatened? Been mistreated? Once, while in the yard, one of the boys threw a stick. "Fetch, Sis, you fast girl!"

Sissy took one look at the stick and ran for the porch. When Shawnelle went to comfort her, the dog's heart was pounding. How could she help the dog feel safe? How could she help Sissy share the love Shawnelle knew was deep inside?

Friday evening was movie night. With snacks in hand, the family started to climb the long, curved staircase to the family room. Sis followed them to the stairwell instead of retreating to the comfort of her crate.

Then she just sat at the bottom. She was afraid of stairs.

"Do you want to come up, Sissy?" Shawnelle asked.

Sis wagged her tail. Gently. Slowly. Barely.

Shawnelle's husband, Lonny, went back down, lifted Sis in his arms, and carried her upstairs. While everyone watched the movie, Sis curled in the closet on a quilt, peering out through the open door. It was the first of many nights the greyhound was carried up to join the family (carried back down, too), and the closet became hers.

One day Shawnelle was stirring soup. Sissy lay at her feet. Shawnelle felt honored that the dog wanted to be with her there, in the quiet moment, just the two of them. When she moved outside, Sis stretched out in the sun. Shawnelle felt a lump in her throat—had Sis ever rested in the sun in her racing life?

Another day, the boys were outside climbing trees. Sissy waited at the bottom. Once, Isaiah fell from the ladder on the clubhouse. By the time Shawnelle heard his cries and raced out of the house, Sis was already on the scene. Isaiah was on the ground, crying. Sissy stood above him, head pressed to his shoulder.

"It's okay, Mom," Isaiah sniffled. "Sissy's making sure I'm all right."

Sissy had become a gentle, quiet presence in their home. She never barked or demanded attention or whined. She never jumped on the children or tried to sneak onto the sofa. She just moved among them, like an angel. Gently watching over them, and often joining in.

Then came the family movie night Shawnelle would never forget. The boys had used their allowances to buy Sissy some toys. They called her to the family room. "Sissy! Come here, girl!"

Lonny turned to go back down the stairs to get her. Then, they heard a noise. Toenails on the wood floor. A gentle scuffling. Sissy bounded up the steps!

"Yay, Sissy, you did it!" the younger boys cheered.

Gabriel opened a package of treats and put a piece on his open-palmed hand. Sissy hesitated. "It's okay, Sis," he said.

And at last, Sissy took the treat. The boys surrounded her with hugs and kisses. Sissy touched them with her wet nose.

Shawnelle turned so the boys didn't see the tears in her eyes. Sis had learned to trust. To have faith in the family. To allow herself to be comfortable and secure. At the same time, the family had learned to be patient. To offer compassion and tenderness.

Shawnelle had once looked into the eyes of a scared, reserved, timid dog. But she'd seen something else. Sis's eyes revealed a hope that went deep. And from that secret well, in time, came a most precious kind of love.

My favorite poem reveals how much we love our dogs, and how we can replace grief with the legacy of love. I share it with all my friends when they lose a pet, and they tell me it brings them as much comfort as it has brought me over the years.

A DOG'S LAST WILL AND TESTAMENT

Before humans die, they write their last will and testament, giving their home and all they have to those they leave behind. If, with my paws, I could do the same, this is what I'd ask . . .

To a poor and lonely stray I'd give my happy home; my bowl and cozy bed, soft pillow and all my toys; the lap, which I loved so much; the hand that stroked my fur; and the sweet voice that spoke my name.

I'd will to the sad, scared shelter dog the place I had in my human's loving heart, of which there seemed no bounds.

So, when I die, please do not say, "I will never have a pet again, for the loss and the pain is more than I can stand."

Instead, go find an unloved dog, one whose life has held no joy or hope, and give my place to him.

This is the only thing I can give . . . the love I left behind.

—AUTHOR UNKNOWN

After we lost our golden retriever, Brooks, we struggled with the decision of whether or not to get a new dog. We'd adopted Brooks when he was eleven years old, and he'd immediately touched our hearts. When cancer took him less than a year later, my husband and I were devastated. I don't think I've ever cried such gut-wrenching sobs for another dog, and I've loved them all deeply. Brooks was special.

Getting a new pet never means replacing the old. No dog would replace Brooks. No dog could ever look at me with the same soulful gaze, sprawl across my chair with the same agility, or love me the exact same way. No dog could be as sweet and gentle and obliging in just the same way as our Brooks. He left a hole, and nothing would be quite right again until it was filled.

If I waited until I healed from losing Brooks, I'd still be waiting. Besides, there were other dogs out there needing homes, longing for the kind of love and comfort we had to give. A dog who otherwise might be left on the streets or in a shelter. We wanted to give another dog a place in our home and our hearts—even hearts that might still be aching.

So, a few weeks after losing our dear Brooks, my husband and I looked at each other and admitted that when the right dog came along, we were ready. And then we smiled for the first time in a long time.

Carefully, we sought out dogs who would get along with our bossy spaniel, Kelly. We considered a puppy. We thought about getting another senior dog. I didn't want to face the possibility of losing another dog again so soon. Then again, a senior dog has so much to offer. I thought maybe my heart was able to handle it again.

After searching, and wondering, and meeting dogs, finally we were introduced to an eight-year-old, skinny golden retriever with patchy fur. He jumped out of the car and pulled at his bright red leash, his tongue hanging out a mile.

And now we have Ike.

And we're in love.

There is a bond that connects us as he greets us with kisses, and runs after the balls we throw, and willingly jumps in the car to go to the vet's. The bond is there when he stops chasing a squirrel when we call "no" even though every fiber of every muscle twinges at the thought of the chase. The bond is there even when he licks where he shouldn't, and slobbers his food, and chews the leg of our new sofa. When he runs, rolls, wags, and sleeps by our feet—that bond is there forever strong and meaningful and beautiful, because we are lucky enough to share our lives with a pet.

Ike's love is simple, warm, and uncomplicated. He puts his paws on my lap like a hug. I tell him he's a good boy. And I hug him back, closing the circle.

O give thanks to the LORD, for he is good;
for his steadfast love endures forever!

PSALM 107:1 NRSV

ACKNOWLEDGMENTS

A special thank you to everyone who shared their amazing and inspiring stories in this book. To pet bloggers Border collie and Hermit (http://slvhermit.tumblr.com), Bringing up Bella (http://www.bringingupbella.com), Family Grace (http://shawnelle writes.blogspot.com), Joyful Paws (http://joyful-paws.com), Melissa's mochas, mysteries & meows (http://www.mochasmys teriesmeows.com), NEPA Pets (http://www.nepa-pets.com), Playful Kitty (http://www.playfulkitty.net), Pooch Smooches (http://www.poochsmooches.com), Something Wagging this way Comes (http://www.somethingwagging.com), and Windows on a Texas Wildscape (http://sherylsmithrodgers.blogspot.com). To Jon Sweeney and the folks at Paraclete Press. Thank you to my wonderful family—a family that has always included dogs, cats, guinea pigs, rabbits, and other furry critters. To my critiquers: Mike Frezon, Kate Fenner, Jackie Bouchard, Susan Karas, and Catherine Madera.

RESOURCES

4 Paws for Ability	http://4pawsforability.org
Alliance for Contraception in Cats and Dogs	http://acc-d.org/
Amazon CARES	http://amazoncares.blogspot.com
American Society for the Prevention of Cruelty to Animals	https://www.aspca.org
Canine Assistants	http://www.canineassistants.org
Canine Good Citizen Program	http://www.akc.org/dog-owners/training/
Caring for Critters	http://www.heartlikeadog.com/community-page
Combat Canines	http://www.combatcanines.org
Earthshine Nature	http://www.earthshinenature.com
Farm Sanctuary	http://www.farmsanctuary.org
Guide Dogs for the Blind	http://welcome.guidedogs.com
Healing Heart Sanctuary	http://healingheartsanctuary.org
Hope for Paws	http://www.hopeforpaws.org
Jasper Ridge Farm	http://www.rileys-place.org
K9 Fit Club	http://k9fitclub.com
Keep Kids Fire Safe	http://www.firesafetyrocks.com
Living with a Blind Cat	http://www.gwencooper.com/living-with-a-blind-cat
Marine Animal Rescue	http://www.marspecialists.org
Morris Animal Foundation	http://www.morrisanimalfoundation.org
My Name Is Lentil	http://www.mynameislentil.com/index.html
National Walk 'n' Roll Dog Day	http://nationalwalknrolldogday.com
Operation Migration	http://www.operationmigration.org
Paws for Purple Hearts	http://www.pawsforpurplehearts.org

Peppertree Rescue	http://www.peppertree.org
Petfinder	https://www.petfinder.com
Pets Are Like Family	http://petsarelikefamily.org
Pine Street Foundation	http://pinestreetfoundation.org
Puppies Behind Bars	http://www.puppiesbehindbars.com/home
Rocky Ridge Refuge	http://rockyridgerefuge.com/about
Silver Paw Ranch	http://www.silverpawranch.com
Stonehouse Photography	http://stonehousephotoblog.com travel-sessions-and-shelters
Take Your Dog to Work Day	http://www.takeyourdog.com
The Elephant Sanctuary	http://www.elephants.com
The Humane Society of the United States	http://www.humanesociety.org
The Xerces Society	http://www.xerces.org
Therapy Dogs International	http://www.tdi-dog.org
Trails Carolina	http://trailscarolina.com
Ugly Animal Preservation Society	http://uglyanimalsoc.com
William Berloni Theatrical Animals	http://www.theatricalanimals.com

REFERENCES

"7 incredibly loyal dogs." Accessed November 19, 2014. http://www.mnn.com/family/pets/photos/7-incredibly-loyal-dogs/hachiko.

The American Kennel Club. "Get to know the Akita." Accessed November 19, 2014. http://www.akc.org/breeds/akita/index.cfm.

American Society for the Prevention of Cruelty to Animals. Accessed November 19, 2014. http://www.aspca.org/.

"American Veterinary Medical Association." Accessed November 18, 2014. https://www.avma.org/Pages/home.aspx.

Angier, Natalie. "The Creature Connection." Last modified March 14, 2011. http://www.nytimes.com/2011/03/15/science/15why.html.

Animal Health Foundation. "Universal Human-Animal Bond Scale." Accessed November 18, 2014. http://www.animalhealthfoundation.net/downloads/HAB%20Scale.pdf.

Aurand-Mayes, Annie. "The Compassion of a Cat Named Bird." Last modified March 3, 2010. http://lovemeow.com/2010/03/the-compassion-of-a-cat-named-bird/.

Bindley, Katherine. "Holly, Lost Cat, Travels 190 Miles Home to Owners." Last modified January 16, 2013. http://www.huffingtonpost.com/2013/01/14/holly-lost-cat_n_2473952.html.

Binette, Karen Harrison. "Firefighters Rescue Tiny Kittens Then Save Them from Euthanasia." Last modified May 7, 2013. http://www.lifewithcats.tv/2013/05/07firefighters-rescue-tiny-kittens-then-save-them-from-euthanasia/.

"Blind Dog and Her Seeing Eye Dog." Accessed December 2, 2014. http://www.foxnews.com/world/2011/10/24/blind-dog-and-her-seeing-eye-dog-looking-for -home/.

"Bobbie the Wonder Dog." Accessed November 19, 2014. http://en.wikipedia.org/wiki/Bobbie_the_Wonder_Dog.

"Bobby's Vigil." Accessed November 19, 2014. http://greyfriarsbobby.co.uk /vigil.html.

Boks, Ed. "New study focuses on human-animal bond." Last modified January 15, 2014. http://www.dcourier.com/main.asp?SectionID=1&SubSectionID=1& ArticleID=127377.

Canine Lifetime Health Project. Accessed November 19, 2014. http://www .caninelifetimehealth.org/for-golden-retriever-dog-lovers/.

CBS Interactive Inc. "Colorado's Flood Rescue: 'No Pets Left Behind'." Last modified September 20, 2013. http://www.cbsnews.com/news/ colorados-flood-rescue-no-pets-left-behind/.

Celizic, Mike. "Hero Dog Brings Help to Burning Home." Last modified April 23, 2013. http://www.today.com/id/36733102/ns/today-today_pets/t/ hero-dog-brings-help-burning-home/.

Centers for Disease Control and Prevention. "FastStats—Obesity and Overweight." Last modified May 14, 2014. http://www.cdc.gov/nchs/fastats/ obesity-overweight.htm.

Centers for Disease Control and Prevention. "Health Benefits of Pets." Accessed November 19, 2014. http://www.cdc.gov/healthypets/health-benefits/ .

CNBC. "10 Companies That Let You Bring Your Dog to Work." Accessed November 19, 2014. http://www.cnbc.com/id/101396437.

Coffey, Laura. "Dog Who Saved Owner on 9/11 Named American Hero Dog." Last modified October 3, 2011. http://www.today.com/id/44615382/ns/ today-today_pets/t/dog-who-saved-owner-named-american-hero-dog/.

Cooper, Gwen. *Homer's Odyssey: A Fearless Feline Tale, or How I Learned about Love and Life with a Blind Wonder Cat.* New York: Delacorte Press, 2009.

Coren, Stanley. "Can Dogs Form True Friendships with Other Dogs?" Last modified February 18, 2013. http://www.psychologytoday.com/blog/canine-corner /201302/can-dogs-form-true-friendships-other-dogs.

Coren, Stanley. "Stanley Coren, Ph.D., F.R.S.C." Accessed November 18, 2014, http://www.psychologytoday.com/experts/stanley-coren-phd-frsc.

Cushing, Mark. "Human-Animal Bond Goes Mainstream in the *Wall Street Journal*." Last modified December 17, 2013. http://veterinarynews.dvm360.com /dvm/Veterinary+news/Blog-Human-animal-bond-goes-mainstream-in-the -iWal/ArticleStandard/Article/detail/831151?contextCategoryId=378.

"Deer, Goose Form Unlikely Friendship." Last modified June 8, 2011. http:// www.huffingtonpost.com/2011/04/08/deer-goose-video_n_846542.html.

"Desperate Dog Sneaks out to Find Owner at L.I. Hospital." Last modified October 4, 2012. http://newyork.cbslocal.com/2012/10/04/desperate-dog-sneaks-out-to-find-owner-at-l-i-hospital/.

Dirks, Leland and Angelo. *Angelo's Journey: A Border Collie's Quest for Home*. CreateSpace, 2011.

"Dominic the Pit Bull Puppy Cuddles and Comforts Animal Patients at Colorado Veterinary Clinic." Last modified December 30, 2013. http://www. huffingtonpost.com/2013/12/23/dominic-comfort-pit-bull-_n_4468767.html.

"Echo: An Elephant to Remember." Last modified October 11, 2010. http:// www.pbs.org/wnet/nature/episodes/echo-an-elephant-to-remember/elephant -emotions/4489/.

Ehrenfreund, Max. "Cat Saved Several People from Flooding in Estes Park, Colo." Last modified September 16, 2013. http://www.washingtonpost.com/ national/cat-saved-several-people-from-flooding-in-estes-park-colo/2013/09 /16/9382e0b2-1f02-11e3-8459-657e0c72fec8_story.html.

"Filippo the Dolphin Saves Italian Boy from Drowning." Last modified August 29, 2000. http://articles.orlandosentinel.com/2000-08-29/news/0008290092_ 1_manfredonia-dolphin-adriatic-sea.

Flowers, Amy. "27 Ways Pets Can Improve Your Health." Last modified October 21, 2014. http://pets.webmd.com/ss/slideshow-pets-improve-your-health.

Frey, David. "Therapy Farm Animals Provide Comfort to the Sick and Elderly." Accessed November 19, 2014. http://www.tractorsupply.com/know-how _Livestock-Care-General_therapy-farm-animals-provide-comfort-to-the-sick-and-elderly.

Frezon, Peggy. "A Dog's Nose Knows How to Sniff Out Disease." http://w www
.guideposts.org/pet-stories/a-dogs-nose-knows-how-to-sniff-out-disease.

Fuoco, Michael. "Oinking for Help." Last modified October 10, 1998. http://
old.post-gazette.com/regionstate/19981010pig2.asp.

Gilani, Nadia. "Hero Dog Drags His Owner Home after He Is Knocked
Unconscious by Lightning Bolt." Last modified October 28, 2011. http://
www.dailymail.co.uk/news/article-2054488/Faithful-dog-drags-owner-hit
-lightening-bolt-home-safety.html.

"Guide Dog Graduates UMass Boston with Student." Last modified May 31,
2014. http://www.myfoxboston.com/story/25644158/guide-dog-to-graduate
-umass-boston-with-student.

Hartman, Steve. "On Elephant Sanctuary, Unlikely Friends." Last modified
January 2, 2009. http://www.cbsnews.com/stories/2009/01/02/assignment
_america/main4696340.shtml.

Healing Heart Sanctuary. Accessed November 19, 2014. http://healingheart
sanctuary.org/programs/healing_children/index.html.

Hope for Paws. Accessed November 19, 2014. http://www.hopeforpaws.org/
home.

"Jambo the Gentle Giant: The Incredible Story." Accessed November 19,
2014. http://lelion.co.uk/.

"Kids Comfort Shelter Animals by Reading to Them." Accessed November
19, 2014. http://www.huffingtonpost.com/tag/kids-comfort-shelter-animals
-by-reading-to-them.

Lishman, William. "Flight with Birds." Accessed November 19, 2014. http://
www.williamlishman.com/flight_with_birds.htm.

"Man and Goose: An L.A. Love Story." Last modified February 11, 2011. http://
live.wsj.com/video/man-and-goose-an-la-love-story/BE713670-1098-4B78
-B3F1-08FDFB4B7A98. html#!BE713670-1098-4B78-B3F1-08FDFB4B7A98.

Mott, Maryanne. "Seizure-Alert Dogs Save Humans with Early Warnings." Last modified February 11, 2004. http://news.nationalgeographic.com/news/2003/04/0416_030416_seizuredogs.html.

National Geographic. "Eye of the Leopard." Accessed November 19, 2014. http://channel.nationalgeographic.com/wild/episodes/eye-of-the-leopard/.

National Institute of Health. "Can Pets Help Keep You Healthy?" Accessed November 19, 2014. http://newsinhealth.nih.gov/2009/February/feature1.htm.

"Neuroscientist Uses MRI Scans to Show That Dogs Have Emotions Similar to Humans." Last modified October 8, 2013. http://www.foxnews.com/health/2013/10/08/neuroscientist-uses-mri-scans-to-show-that-dogs-have-emotions-similar-to-humans.

O'Callaghan, Tiffany. "Forget Pandas—Ugly Animals Should Be Protected Too." Last modified June 24, 2013. http://www.newscientist.com/article/mg21829220.300-forget-pandas-ugly-animals-should-be-protected-too.html.

Pets Are Like Family. Accessed November 19, 2014. http://petsarelikefamily.org/.

"Prayer of a Stray." Accessed November 19, 2014. http://www.alterpet.org/pet_poems.htm.

Take Your Dog to Work Day. Accessed November 19, 2014. http://www.takeyourdog.com/About/.

Trails Carolina. Accessed November 19, 2014. http://www.TrailsCarolina.com.

Vang, Gia. "Rats for Pet Therapy—Yes, Really." Last modified March 12, 2013. http://fox4kc.com/2013/03/12/rats-for-pet-therapy-yes-really/.

Villarica, Hans. "Dog Walkers Get More Exercise." Last modified March 16, 2011. http://healthland.time.com/2011/03/16/cue-the-canine-dog-walkers-are-more-likely-to-reach-fitness-goals-study-says/.

Yune, Howard. "Bomb Dogs to Protect Napa Valley Marathon." Last modified February 27, 2014. http://napavalleyregister.com/news/local/bomb-dog-to-protect-napa-valley-marathon/article_c3caa5b2-a011-11e3-b4bd-0019bb2963f4.html.

NOTES

1. Stanley Coren, "Can Dogs Form True Friendships with Other Dogs?" http://www.psychologytoday.com/blog/canine-corner/201302/can-dogs-form-true-friendships-other-dogs.

2. Leland and Angelo Dirks, *Angelo's Journey: A Border Collie's Quest for Home* (CreateSpace, 2011).

3. Thomas O. Chisholm, "Great Is Thy Faithfulness." Tune: Faithfulness, by William M. Runyan.

4. "Prayer of a Stray," http://www.alterpet.org/pet_poems.htm.

5. Peggy Frezon, "A Dog's Nose Knows How to Sniff Out Disease," http://www.guideposts.org/pet-stories/a-dogs-nose-knows-how-to-sniff-out-disease.

6. Ibid.

7. Gwen Cooper, *Homer's Odyssey: A Fearless Feline Tale, or How I Learned about Love and Life with a Blind Wonder Cat* (New York: Delacorte Press, 2009).

ABOUT PARACLETE PRESS

WHO WE ARE

Paraclete Press is a publisher of books, recordings, and DVDs on Christian spirituality. Our publishing represents a full expression of Christian belief and practice—from Catholic to Evangelical, from Protestant to Orthodox.

We are the publishing arm of the Community of Jesus, an ecumenical monastic community in the Benedictine tradition. As such, we are uniquely positioned in the marketplace without connection to a large corporation and with informal relationships to many branches and denominations of faith.

WHAT WE ARE DOING

PARACLETE PRESS BOOKS | Paraclete publishes books that show the richness and depth of what it means to be Christian. Although Benedictine spirituality is at the heart of all that we do, we publish books that reflect the Christian experience across many cultures, time periods, and houses of worship. We publish books that nourish the vibrant life of the church and its people.

We have several different series, including the best-selling Paraclete Essentials and Paraclete Giants series of classic texts in contemporary English; Voices from the Monastery—men and women monastics writing about living a spiritual life today; award-winning poetry; best-selling gift books for children on the occasions of baptism and first communion; and the Active Prayer Series that brings creativity and liveliness to any life of prayer.

MOUNT TABOR BOOKS | Paraclete's newest series, Mount Tabor Books, focuses on liturgical worship, art and art history, ecumenism, and the first millennium church, and was created in conjunction with the Mount Tabor Ecumenical Centre for Art and Spirituality in Barga, Italy.

PARACLETE RECORDINGS | From Gregorian chant to contemporary American choral works, our recordings celebrate the best of sacred choral music composed through the centuries that create a space for heaven and earth to intersect. Paraclete Recordings is the record label representing the internationally acclaimed choir Gloriæ Dei Cantores, praised for their "rapt and fathomless spiritual intensity" by *American Record Guide*; the Gloriæ Dei Cantores Schola, specializing in the study and performance of Gregorian chant; and the other instrumental artists of the Gloriæ Dei Artes Foundation.

Paraclete Press is also privileged to be the exclusive North American distributor of the recordings of the Monastic Choir of St. Peter's Abbey in Solesmes, France, long considered to be a leading authority on Gregorian chant.

PARACLETE VIDEO | Our DVDs offer spiritual help, healing, and biblical guidance for a broad range of life issues including grief and loss, marriage, forgiveness, facing death, bullying, addictions, Alzheimer's, and spiritual formation.

Learn more about us at our website:
www.paracletepress.com or phone us
toll-free at 1.800.451.5006

SCAN
TO
READ
MORE

Also available from Paraclete Press...

Will I See My Dog in Heaven?
God's Saving Love for the Whole Family of Creation
Jack Wintz
ISBN: 978-1-55725-568-6 $14.99, Paperback

Father Jack admits that no one really knows what God has in mind for us in the next life. But in ten thoughtful chapters, he lines up evidence from the Scriptures, Christian tradition and liturgy, and the life and teachings of St. Francis of Assisi, that God desires all creatures (yes, including our beloved pets!) in the afterlife.

All God's Creatures:
The Blessing of Animal Companions
Debra K. Farrington
ISBN: 978-1-55725-472-6, $15.99, Paperback

Full of warmth and wisdom, this book explores the spiritual aspects of our relationships with these beloved friends—from everyday caring for their needs, to marking the extraordinary moments of birth, illness, and death.

I Will See You in Heaven
Jack Wintz
ISBN: 978-1-55725-732-1, $14.99, Hardcover

For anyone who is grieving the loss of beloved pets, this bestselling little book offers wisdom, comfort, and the reassuring hope that we will see our cats and dogs and other animals in heaven.